Managing Performance:

Performance management in action

Michael Armstrong graduated from the London School of Economics, and is a Companion of the Chartered Institute of Personnel and Development and a Fellow of the Institute of Management Consultants. He has had over 25 years' experience in personnel management, including 12 as a personnel director. He has also practised as a management consultant for 16 years and was formerly chief examiner, employee reward, for the CIPD. He has written a number of successful management books, including *The Job Evaluation Handbook* (1995, with Angela Baron), *Employee Reward* (2002) and *New Dimensions in Pay Management* (2001, with Duncan Brown). All are published by the CIPD.

Angela Baron has been Adviser, Organisation and Resourcing at the Chartered Institute of Personnel and Development since 1990. She is currently managing the CIPD's work on HR and business performance and human capital reporting. Angela's previous books include *The Job Evaluation Handbook*, and *Strategic HRM* both co-written with Michael Armstrong. She holds a Masters degree in Occupational and Organisational Psychology and is a Chartered member of the CIPD.

The Chartered Institute of Personnel and Development is the
leading publisher of books and reports for personnel and training
professionals, students, and all those concerned with the effective
management and development of people at work. For details of all
our titles, please contact the publishing department:

tel: 020-8263 3387

fax: 020-8263 3850

e-mail publish@cipd.co.uk

The catalogue of all CIPD titles can be viewed on the CIPD website:
www.cipd.co.uk/bookstore

Managing Performance:

Performance management in action

Michael Armstrong
Angela Baron

Chartered Institute of Personnel and Development

Published by the Chartered Institute of Personnel and Development,
CIPD House, Camp Road, London, SW19 4UX

First edition published 2005

Design by Beacon GDT, Mitcheldean, Gloucestershire
Typeset by Fakenham Photosetting Ltd, Fakenham, Norfolk
Printed in Great Britain by The Cromwell Press, Trowbridge, Wiltshire

British Library Cataloguing in Publication Data
A catalogue of this publication is available from the British Library

ISBN 1 84398 101 7

Chartered Institute of Personnel and Development, CIPD House,
Camp Road, London, SW19 4UX
Tel: 020 8971 9000   Fax: 020 8263 3333
Email: cipd@cipd.co.uk   Website: www.cipd.co.uk
Incorporated by Royal Charter.   Registered Charity No. 1079797

Contents

List of Figures and Tables

Figures

Tables

Foreword

The whole ethos of performance management rests on the assumption that if you can raise the performance levels of individuals, better organisational performance will follow. It was not a surprise, therefore, that the first investigation into performance management carried out by the Institute of Personnel Management in 1991 concluded that performance management was about making sure managers manage properly – that they clearly and consistently communicate to their staff what is expected of them and give them the means to meet that expectation.

Over the years this idea that performance management is a tool for line managers to ensure that they carry out their line management duties effectively has become firmly embedded. All of the individuals interviewed for this book agreed that the success or failure of performance management is down to the line managers. As personnel professionals we can give them the tools but we cannot force them to use them. However, as many of the companies reported on in this book demonstrate, we can positively encourage them to recognise the value of performance management tools in enabling them to do their jobs more effectively and meet their own targets and objectives.

We will only be able to do this if we can offer well designed and articulated tools, together with the development of skills and understanding to enable them to use them to best effect. This area of performance management perhaps more than any other clearly demonstrates the need for personnel professionals to work in partnership with the line to ensure the effective delivery of personnel practices and policies. We know that people make the difference but we are not there every minute of the day to oversee the behaviours and actions that really make the difference on the front line. Previous CIPD research tells us that managers who can motivate their staff to deliver performance above the minimum, can persuade them to go the extra mile to please the customer, can solve the problem or can come up with a new product, make the difference between good companies and great companies.

This book offers practical advice and guidance for practitioners to develop performance management processes that line managers can value and use to deliver performance where it matters. It demonstrates that performance management is a holistic and integrated process which has implications for a broad range of people management policies, and is not just a means of setting and reviewing objectives. It argues that performance management is about ensuring that all the people in our organisations can reach their potential and remain committed and motivated employees.

It is no surprise that performance management has been identified as a key tool for organisational success. The challenge is to ensure that tool is used effectively and is focused on what really matters.

David Smith
People Director, ASDA Stores
CIPD Vice-President, Organisation and Resourcing

1

An overview of performance management

The essential features of performance management are described in this chapter under the following headings:

- performance management defined
- the overall purpose and aims of performance management
- a short history of performance management
- performance management and discretionary behaviour
- performance management and human capital advantage
- performance management questions
- the significance of the concept of performance
- performance management and values
- principles of performance management
- the performance management cycle
- performance management and performance appraisal
- the impact of performance management on organisational performance
- the reactions of employees to performance management
- performance management and HR
- performance management and line managers
- the ethics of performance management
- developments in performance management.

PERFORMANCE MANAGEMENT DEFINED

The term 'performance management' first came into wide use in the HR field in the early 1990s. Although objective-setting, assessment and review, and performance-related pay were becoming common prior to that period, it was not until the late 1980s that organisations started to be concerned with the management of individual performance in a holistic way. Even when the then Institute of Personnel Management first carried out research in the area in 1992 there was confusion over what the term 'performance management' actually meant. For some it was an appraisal process, for others performance-related pay, and yet others defined it in terms of training and development. By the time of our second survey in 1997 there was much more agreement about what the term 'performance management' meant, with a distinct polarisation between those who thought it focused on pay and those who believed it was development-led.

It is now commonly agreed that performance management as a natural process of management contributes to the effective management of individuals and teams to achieve high levels of organisational performance. As such, it establishes shared understanding about what is to be achieved and an approach to leading and developing people which will ensure that it is achieved.

Other definitions of performance management – such as those set out below – also emphasise the systematic nature of the process, its focus on the achievement of shared individual and organisation goals, and the importance of development and support:

- 'a systematic approach to improving individual and team performance in order to achieve organisational goals' (Hendry et al[1])

- 'the development of individuals with competence and commitment, working towards the achievement of shared meaningful objectives within an organisation that supports and encourages their achievement' (Lockett[2])

- 'Performance management is managing the business' (Mohrman and Mohrman[3])

- 'directing and supporting employees to work as effectively and efficiently as possible in line with the needs of the organisation' (Walters[4]).

THE OVERALL PURPOSE AND AIMS OF PERFORMANCE MANAGEMENT

The overall purpose of performance management is to contribute to the achievement of high performance by the organisation and its people. 'High performance' means reaching and exceeding stretching targets for the delivery of productivity, quality, customer service, growth, profits and shareholder value.

Specifically, performance management aims to make the good better, share understanding about what is to be achieved, develop the capacity of people to achieve it, and provide the support and guidance people need to deliver high performance and achieve their full potential to the benefit of themselves and the organisation.

Performance management is concerned with under-performers, but it does this positively by providing the means for people to improve their performance or make better use of their abilities.

Examples of performance management aims, philosophies and approaches

Centrica

Joe Dugdale, HR Director, Centrica Telecommunications, told us that:

Our aim throughout the organisation is to manage performance against individual objectives and team objectives where appropriate. Because of the diversity of our business we have deliberately not suggested that there is a single performance management process that can be applied throughout the business. So whilst the principal aims generally apply, the specifics will vary from business to business. One of our principal aims is to encourage managers to focus on whole-job performance. We need to get them away from a focus on achieving an objective that will trigger a reward. It's a big shift in philosophy that it's not just what you do but how you do it that is important.

Education sector

Our interviewee said that performance management should be a tool for line managers to manage properly – to make sure that people are aware of what is expected of them and how to do it.

We are trying to use the management development process to educate managers on the value of actually having on-going performance-type discussions with the people they manage, and as part of this we are trying to develop a people-oriented ethos within the school and a culture that brings out the best in people – trying to create a nice place to work, a place where people enjoy coming to work. This is the central plank of our strategy, to encourage better management behaviours and also to create an environment within which we can retain bright, well-motivated people.

Another education manager strongly believed that the Investors in People accreditation had given them a head start in terms of developing a performance-led culture and in terms of getting performance management embedded and accepted within the college.

Cranfield University

The aims of performance management at Cranfield University were expressed by Ruth Altman, Director, HR and Development:

We are trying to look at how we change the culture, get the buy-in, and sell the benefit of looking at your performance to individuals themselves and encourage them to stand back and evaluate what they are contributing.

First Direct

Jane Hanson, Organisation Development Manager, said to us that at First Direct,

Performance management links in terms of cascading business goals and plans into individual performance and objectives.

GMAC

At GMAC RFC, one of the UK's leading mortgage lenders, Val Ward – Head of Learning and Development – told us that:

> *We have had to move from a process-driven form of performance management linked to objectives to a system aligned to performance and reward. That has been a big culture change. Managers really need to understand the strategy because they have to interpret it to their staff. The strategy emanates from the Enterprise, which is the whole of the business across the world, and then cascades into the UK strategy. This is then fed down to the department and ultimately to individuals.*

Halifax Bank of Scotland Retail

Julie Hill, HR Partner, Retail Sales, Retail Development and HEA Central Sites, informed us that:

> *The essence of the HBOS Retail approach to performance management is that we are looking at how people perform not only against the requirements of the role but also in the way they do it. We are trying to get people that are good at the people skills as well as the deliverables. The system has been put together to make sure we do that, and try and move away from ticking boxes to make it a more meaningful conversation, identifying where an individual is doing well and where he or she is doing less well.*

Norwich Union Insurance

We were told by Marie Sigsworth, Director of HR Customer Service, that:

> *Our ultimate aim is to become an outperforming service provider through a prioritised and sequenced set of interventions. The challenges we face in achieving this are as follows:*

- understanding the minimum number of key levers/outputs that will deliver the desired outcomes
- developing people management and organisational stewardship skills which ensure that staff are fully productive and motivated to perform
- focusing managers and staff on key outputs in a way that drives prioritised action to improve processes and inputs
- developing change competencies that will maximise the effectiveness of all change activity
- understanding the types and level of other competencies required in the organisation
- improving the communications climate, both vertically and horizontally.

NPower

Alec Rudd, Learning and Development Manager of NPower, explained that:

We needed one performance management system across all of the business to ensure that NPower met its targets. This was not 'not nice to have'. We would have been out of business without it. We were looking for a process to create one culture and link performance management to strategy.

Communications

Our interviewee said to us that:

Our key objective is to engender a performance management culture where people recognise they have to perform, that managers recognise performance is key – where people realise it makes a difference and they need to do it. It's not just about ratings, it's about ensuring that people know where they are going.

Rebus HR (now part of Northgate Information Solutions)

Jan Paxton, Senior HR Product Strategy Manager, said that the Rebus performance management strategy was for it to act as a dashboard that drove everything else within the business:

We have this strategic vision in which every single person would have a dashboard on their PC and through that be able to click on to a web of HR polices, initiatives and strategies. One of these would be performance management, so people could at a press of a button look at their own role descriptions, look at their competencies, and look around at the organisation and say, 'That's what I'd actually like to do in three years' time.'

Royal Free Hampstead NHS Trust

Nigel Turner, Director of Human Resources, stated to us that:

Our performance management system is driven both by the importance of providing the best possible services to patients and by the importance of developing staff to have the skills that they need both to deliver the service today and to develop them for tomorrow.

Scottish Parliament

At the Scottish Parliament, performance management is defined in the following terms:

- Ensure that what we do is guided by our values and is relevant to the purposes of the organisation.
- Ensure that we are all clear how to demonstrate the skills, knowledge and behaviours that are expected of us.
- Ensure that we are clear what our individual role is, and how we intend to fulfil it.

- Link our job roles and individual objectives to the organisational objectives and priorities set out in the Management Plan.

- Ensure that all managers agree and review objectives, priorities and developmental needs with team members.

- Review performance against objectives and areas of competence to ensure that we are making the best possible contribution to the organisation's overall aim.

- Ensure that all team members receive constructive feedback in order to develop and improve performance.

- Ensure that a thorough review of training and development takes place as an integral part of the system so that PDPs reflect both business and individual aims.

- Ensure that poor performance is identified quickly and support is provided to eliminate it.

Standard Chartered Bank

Caroline Sharkey, Organisation Development Manager, Standard Chartered Bank, told us about their approach to performance management:

- 'Set a climate in which high management performance is seen to be important.'

- 'The emphasis is on "managing for excellence" – helping people understand what excellence means and how they can achieve it.'

- 'Set objectives which play to people's strengths.'

- 'Each year there has to be a build-up of stretch in objectives, with everyone looking to "raise the bar".'

- 'The first crucial question is: "How do we get people to do their best every day within the objectives they are set?"'

- 'The second crucial question is: "How can we get people to go from good to great?"'

- 'Performance management is all about behaviour.'

A SHORT HISTORY OF PERFORMANCE MANAGEMENT

No one knows precisely when formal methods of reviewing performance were first introduced. It is said that the emperors of the Wei dynasty (AD 221–265) had an 'imperial rater' whose task it was to evaluate the performance of the official family. Centuries later, Ignatius Loyola established a system for formal rating of the members of the Jesuit Society.

The first formal monitoring systems, however, evolved out of the work of Frederick Taylor and his followers before World War I. Rating for officers in the US armed services was introduced in the 1920s, and this then spread to the UK, as did some of the factory-based American systems. Merit rating came to the fore in the USA and the UK in the 1950s and 1960s, when it was sometimes re-christened 'performance appraisal'. Management by objectives then came and went in the 1960s and 1970s, and experiments were made simultaneously with the critical incident technique and behaviourally anchored rating scales. A revised form of results-oriented performance appraisal emerged in the 1970s and still exists today.

The term 'performance management' was first used in the 1970s by Beer and Ruh.[5] Their thesis was that 'Performance is best developed through practical challenges and experiences on the job, with guidance and feedback from superiors.' However, it did not become a recognised process until the latter half of the 1980s. This was confirmed by the research project conducted by the Institute of Personnel Management in 1992,[6] which produced the following definition of performance management:

> *A strategy which relates to every activity of the organisation set in the context of its human resources policies, culture, style and communications systems. The nature of the strategy depends on the organisational context and can vary from organisation to organisation.*

It was suggested that what was described as a 'performance management system' (PMS) complied with the textbook definition when the organisation demonstrated certain characteristics:

- It communicated a vision of its objectives to all its employees.
- It set departmental and individual performance targets which were related to wider objectives.
- It conducted a formal review of progress towards these targets.
- It used the review process to identify training, development and reward outcomes.
- It evaluated the whole process in order to improve effectiveness.
- It used formal appraisal procedures as ways of communicating performance requirements which were set on a regular basis.

The 1992 research found that in the organisations with performance management systems, 85 per cent had performance-related pay (this can be compared with the 31 per cent of respondents to the CIPD 2003 survey with performance-related pay) and 76 per cent rated performance (59 per cent in 2003). The emphasis was on objective-setting and review which, as the authors of the report noted,

> *leaves something of a void when it comes to identifying development needs on a longer-term basis ... There is a danger with results-oriented schemes in focusing excessively on what is to be achieved and ignoring the how.*

It was further noted that some organisations were moving in the direction of competency analysis, but not very systematically.

Two of the IPM researchers (Bevan and Thompson[7]) commented on the emergence of performance management systems as integrating processes which mesh various human resource management activities with the business objectives of the organisation. They identified two broad thrusts towards integration:

- *reward-driven integration*, which emphasises the role of performance pay in changing organisational behaviour and tends to undervalue the part played by other human resource development activities. This appeared to be the dominant mode of integration

- *development-driven integration,* which stresses the importance of HRD. Although performance pay may operate in these organisations, it is perceived to be complementary to HRD activities rather than to dominate them.

Since 1992, the CIPD research projects in 1997[8] and 2003/2004 as reported on in this book have noted the development of the full process of performance management described in this chapter.

PERFORMANCE MANAGEMENT AND DISCRETIONARY BEHAVIOUR

Performance management is concerned with the encouragement of productive discretionary behaviour. As defined by Purcell and his team at Bath University School of Management,[9]

> *Discretionary behaviour refers to the choices that people make about how they carry out their work and the amount of effort, care, innovation and productive behaviour they display. It is the difference between people just doing a job and people doing a great job.*

Purcell and his team, while researching the relationship between HR practice and business performance, noted that 'The experience of success seen in performance outcomes helps reinforce positive attitudes.'

PERFORMANCE MANAGEMENT AND HUMAN CAPITAL ADVANTAGE

Ultimately, the goal of performance management is to achieve human capital advantage. People are now recognised as the most important source of competitive advantage. As opposed to other forms of competitive advantage resulting from improvements in factors such as design or process, the 'people factor' is difficult to replicate, which makes it extremely valuable to organisations. As described by Boxall,[10] human capital advantage results from employing people with competitively valuable knowledge and skills. It means developing the organisation's intellectual capital – 'the accumulated stock of knowledge, skills and abilities that individuals possess which the firm has built up over time as identifiable expertise' (Kamoche[11]). To achieve this, performance management has to be integrated with the key HR processes of resourcing, human resource development and knowledge management. It must also be delivered by managers with the necessary understanding about the contribution of the business that will enable them to develop the skills and behaviours to maximise this advantage.

PERFORMANCE MANAGEMENT QUESTIONS

To develop and maintain effective performance management processes the following questions should be answered:

— starting point

1 What do we mean by 'high performance'?

2 Do our people understand what is expected of them in terms of performance?

3 How can we align individual and corporate objectives?

4 To what extent is performance management about supporting the core values of the organisation?

5 Can we identify good and poor performance?

6 Can we establish the reasons for good or not so good performance?

7 How can we develop and motivate people to perform well?

8 How can we do all that fairly, consistently, and without discrimination?

THE SIGNIFICANCE OF THE CONCEPT OF PERFORMANCE

— quantitative
— qualitative

The questions are all important but the first one is especially significant. Performance is often regarded simply in output terms – the achievement of quantified objectives. But it is more than that: it is the outcomes of activity and endeavour that matter. These can be assessed qualitatively by reference to standards of performance defined in the form 'Performance will meet the required standard when ...'. Outcomes can also, of course, be assessed against quantified targets or goals expressed as projects or tasks to be completed satisfactorily on a one-off or continuing basis.

But performance is a matter not only of what people achieve but of how they achieve it. High performance results from appropriate behaviour, especially discretionary behaviour, and the effective use of the required knowledge, skills and competencies. Performance management must examine how results are attained because this provides the information necessary to consider what needs to be done to improve these results.

PERFORMANCE MANAGEMENT AND VALUES

Performance is about upholding the values of the organisation – 'living the values' (an approach to which much importance was attached at Standard Chartered Bank). This is an aspect of behaviour but it focuses on what people do to realise core values such as concern for quality, concern for people, concern for equal opportunity and operating ethically. It means converting espoused values into values in use: ensuring that the rhetoric becomes reality. The focus on values was a marked feature in many of the organisations we visited during our field research, and is one of the major developments since our last research project.

At GMAC RFC, Val Ward, Head of Learning and Development, explained to us that:

> *The what we do is linked to our vision from which flows our strategy and objectives, but the how we do it is embedded in our values and operating principles, and these are translated into the expected performance behaviours ... People are rated on performance behaviours just as they are with objectives. They are asked to supply any evidence, anecdotes, letters of commendation etc ... It's about what else you do, not just reaching sales targets. So we don't want people reaching their objectives but at the expense of the team ethos.*

At First Direct Jane Hanson, Organisation Development Manager, explained that:

> *We have just developed a specific objective this year that's around the First Direct core values and is applied to anybody who manages or leads people. It's about them acting as role models, displaying positive behaviour themselves, but it's also about how they encourage others to behave in that way.*

Performance management in the Scottish Parliament is very much concerned with upholding the core values, and staff have been informed that:

> *Our success depends on all of us sharing the common values set out in the management plan, ie:*

Integrity	*We demonstrate high standards of honesty and reliability.*
Impartiality	*We are fair and even-handed in dealing with members of the public and each other.*
Professionalism	*We provide high-quality professional advice and support services.*
Client focus	*We are responsive to the needs of Members, the public and one another.*
Efficiency	*We use resources responsibility and cost-effectively.*
Mutual respect	*We treat everyone with respect and courtesy and take full account of equal opportunities issues at all times.*

PRINCIPLES OF PERFORMANCE MANAGEMENT

Egan[12] proposes the following guiding principles for performance management:

> *Most employees want direction, freedom to get their work done, and encouragement, not control. The performance management system should be a control system only by exception. The solution is to make it a collaborative development system. In two ways. First, the entire performance management process – coaching, counselling, feedback, tracking, recognition, and so forth – should encourage development. Ideally, team*

members grow and develop through these interactions. Second, when managers and team members ask what they need to be able to do to do bigger and better things, they move to strategic development.

The principles of performance management have also been well summarised by Incomes Data Services:[13]

- It translates corporate goals into individual, team, department and divisional goals.
- It helps to clarify corporate goals.
- It is a continuous and evolutionary process, in which performance improves over time.
- It relies on consensus and co-operation rather than control or coercion.
- It creates a shared understanding of what is required to improve performance and how it will be achieved.
- It encourages self-management of individual performance.
- It requires a management style that is open and honest and encourages two-way communication between superiors and subordinates.
- It requires continuous feedback.
- Feedback loops enable the experiences and knowledge gained on the job by individuals to modify corporate objectives.
- It measures and assesses all performance against jointly agreed goals.
- It should apply to all staff.
- It is not primarily concerned with linking performance to financial reward.

To which could be added that performance management is about providing support as well as direction.

The extensive research conducted by the CIPD in 1997 and 2003/4 (Armstrong and Baron[8]) identified ten maxims from practitioners on how these principles should be applied:

1 'a management tool which helps managers to manage'

2 'driven by corporate purpose and values'

3 'to obtain solutions that work'

4 'only interested in things you can do something about and get a visible improvement'

5 'Focus on changing behaviour rather than paperwork.'

6 'It's about how we manage people – it's not a system.'

7 'Performance management is what managers do: a natural process of management.'

8 'based on accepted principles but operates flexibly'

9 'Focus on development, not pay.'

10 'Success depends on what the organisation is and needs to be in its performance culture.'

Julie Hill, HR Partner, Retail Sales, Retail Development and HEA Central Sites, Halifax Bank of Scotland (HBOS), explained that the principles of their approach to performance management were:

- having a simple process which removes unnecessary paperwork

- establishing simple, clear performance plans

- providing managers with a framework for recognising and differentiating colleagues' individual contribution and rewarding them through devolved pay

- ensuring that any issues around performance shortfalls or capability are resolved

- 'Documentation has to be the exception.'

Julie Hill also pointed out that:

Managing performance is about coaching, guiding, appraising, motivating and rewarding colleagues to help unleash potential and improve organisational performance. Where it works well it is built on excellent leadership and high-quality coaching relationships between managers and teams. Through all this our colleagues should be able to answer three straightforward questions:

1 *What is expected of me?* How will I be clear about what is expected of me in terms of both results and behaviour?

2 *How am I doing?* What ongoing coaching and feedback will I receive to tell me how I am doing, and how I can improve?

3 *What does it mean for me?* How will my individual contribution, potential and aspirations be recognised and rewarded?

Putting the principles into effect

There is no single good or best way of conducting performance management. But the overriding principle is that good performance management is equated with good management. It is about ensuring that managers manage effectively, that they communicate with staff and that they understand what is expected of them, have the capability to deliver it and are motivated to deliver to the highest possible standards. The CIPD research *Understanding the People and Performance Link: Unlocking the black box*[9] carried out by John Purcell and his team at Bath University School of Management concluded that it is not HR practices which build organisational success – it is their delivery in a flexible and positive way by line managers.

THE PERFORMANCE MANAGEMENT CYCLE

Performance management is a natural process of management. It is not an HRM technique or tool. The performance management cycle as shown in Figure 1 corresponds with William Deming's Plan-Do-Check-Act model.[14]

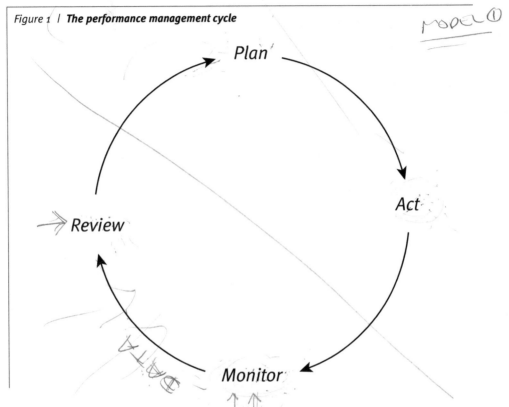

*Figure 1 | **The performance management cycle***

The performance management processes taking place in this cycle are:

- *Plan:* agreeing objectives and competence requirements; identifying the behaviours required by the organisation; producing plans expressed in performance agreements for meeting objectives and improving performance; preparing personal development plans to enhance knowledge, skills and competence and reinforce the desired behaviours

- *Act:* carrying out the work required to achieve objectives by reference to the plans and in response to new demands

- *Monitor:* checking on progress in achieving objectives and responding to new demands; treating performance management as a continuous process – 'managing performance all the year round' – rather than an annual appraisal event

- *Review:* holding a review meeting for a 'stocktaking' assessment of progress and achievements, and identifying where action is required to develop performance as a basis for completing the cycle by moving into the planning stage.

A model of the performance management process used in Chartered Standard Bank is illustrated in Figure 2.

PERFORMANCE MANAGEMENT AND PERFORMANCE APPRAISAL

The terms 'performance management' and 'performance appraisal' are sometimes used synonymously, but they are different. Performance management is a comprehensive, continuous and flexible approach to the management of organisations, teams and individuals which involves the maximum amount of dialogue between those concerned. Performance appraisal is a more limited approach which involves managers making top-down assessments and rating the performance of their subordinates at an annual performance appraisal meeting.

Figure 2 | *Performance management model, Standard Chartered Bank*

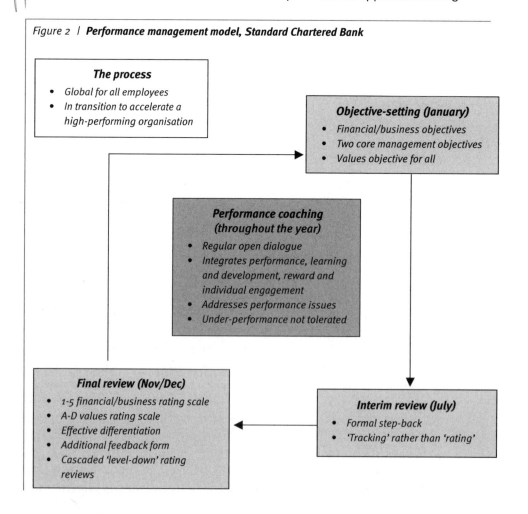

The differences are summarised in Table 1.

Table 1 | Performance appraisal compared with performance management

Performance appraisal	Performance management
Top-down assessment	Joint process through dialogue
Annual appraisal meeting	Continuous review with one or more formal reviews
Use of ratings	Ratings less common
Monolithic system	Flexible process
Focus on quantified objectives	Focus on values and behaviours as well as objectives
Often linked to pay	Less likely to be directly linked to pay
Bureaucratic – complex paperwork	Documentation kept to a minimum
Owned by the HR department	Owned by line managers

THE IMPACT OF PERFORMANCE MANAGEMENT ON ORGANISATIONAL PERFORMANCE

The report on the 1992 IPM[6] research into performance management stated that:

One positive theme which can be traced throughout the research is the extent to which performance management raises awareness of the pressures on the organisation to perform.

The survey conducted by the IPD in 1997 (Armstrong and Baron[8]) established that the 388 respondents with performance management were generally confident that their organisations were mainly in the upper quartile compared with others, especially with regard to quality of goods and service and the workforce.

A large proportion (42 per cent) of the 451 respondents to the 2003/2004 CIPD performance management survey upon which this book is based believe that their performance management processes are very or mostly effective in improving overall performance. A further 49 per cent thought that performance management was partly effective. But only 4 per cent considered that it was ineffective. This is a reasonably strong endorsement of the impact of performance management.

It is, of course, hard to establish causation when investigating the link between any single HR practice and organisational performance. There are too many other factors that get in the way. However, a number of research studies in the USA carried out during the 1990s have identified a link between HR practice and performance (Ichniowski, Shaw and Prennushi,[15] Delery and Doty,[16] Huselid[17]). David Guest[18] concluded on the basis of a UK survey covering 835 organisations that there is a strong positive correlation between the number of HR practices adopted and managers' perceptions of positive employee behaviours and attitudes. In turn, these

Guest

lead to higher productivity, quality of goods and services and financial results. Within all of these studies there was a strong emphasis on the practices associated with the performance management process.

As a result of this work it is now widely accepted that there is a positive relationship between good HR practice and better business performance. Performance management adds value to this relationship because it can:

- communicate a shared vision of the purpose and values of the organisation
- define expectations of what must be delivered and how it should be delivered
- ensure that people are aware of what constitutes high performance and how they need to behave to achieve it
- enhance motivation, engagement and commitment by providing a means of recognising endeavour and achievement through feedback
- provide the basis for formulating personal development and improvement plans
- enable people to monitor their own performance as well as that of those responsible to them against agreed objectives and standards
- encourage dialogue about what needs to be done to improve performance – achieving this by mutual agreement rather than by dictation from above.

THE REACTIONS OF EMPLOYEES TO PERFORMANCE MANAGEMENT

Respondents to our survey believed that 50 per cent of staff felt that performance management was partly effective and 36 per cent felt that it was mostly effective. This is not a full endorsement of performance management and suggests that there is quite a lot of room for improvement. But it does not support the conventional view held generally by many academics that performance management/appraisal processes are universally disliked by people at the receiving end.

The IPD research in 1997[8] found through focus groups in six organisations that on the whole more employees had favourable rather than unfavourable views about performance management. Some of their comments were:

- 'You need appraisal to get the best out of people and develop them.'
- 'What we've moved away from is people's perceptions – just marking someone depending on how they felt about them. Now there's evidence.'
- 'They can tell us what they want, just as we can tell them what we want.'
- 'In a one-to-one meeting, people can bring things out to their supervisors who say "I've never been aware of that: why didn't you tell us before?" That's definitely an advantage.'
- 'If you want to go ahead, if you want to work yourself up, then it's good

because you can find out what your needs are. You can discuss the issues, rather than being told, "That is what you need to be." You can then go away happy, thinking I know what I want to know about that.'

- 'For me the real strength of the process lies in the continuing dialogue and negotiation as the year goes on.'
- 'You're one-to-one with your boss. You've chatted, and it wasn't as if it was your boss. It was more relaxed. He would listen and then you'd chat about it. I enjoyed it.'

Conversely, research by Sue Hutchinson and John Purcell[19] established that the employees in the organisations they studied believed that performance appraisal (not performance management) was rated as the least effective HR policy (in terms of levels of satisfaction) after pay, and in a fair number of organisations it was the least favourite HR activity.

PERFORMANCE MANAGEMENT AND HR

In the past performance appraisal was driven by the personnel department and often seen by line managers as something imposed on them rather than part of the normal process of managing resources. But that does not apply to the performance management approaches identified in our research and described in this book. Performance management is something that line managers do – encouraged, advised and guided by HR, perhaps – but it is managers who are responsible. In the organisations we studied such as Halifax BOS, the Scottish Parliament and Standard Chartered Bank, performance management was a *management* policy which concerned top management as a means of improving organisational performance and was owned by them, not HR. In these and other cases it was not regarded as an HR policy. In one of the organisations we interviewed it was not considered a policy at all but rather a process that managers were encouraged to use to help them manage their staff effectively.

PERFORMANCE MANAGEMENT AND LINE MANAGERS

Performance management is owned and delivered by line managers. It is not a personnel technique run by the HR department. The research conducted by Purcell and his colleagues[9] underlined the importance of line management commitment and capability as the means by which HR policies (or indeed any other corporate policies) are brought to life. An important consideration in designing and operating performance management is how this commitment and capability can be developed.

Julie Hill, HR Partner, Retail Sales, Retail Development and HEA Central Sites, Halifax Bank of Scotland, said that:

Performance management works very well with managers who are competent. Those who are less competent with the behavioural requirements of their role find it difficult, as this approach requires them to make some business judgements and discuss the rationale for them. Previously, they relied on the tick-box approach where there was sometimes a perception that they did not need to discuss performance in detail. We have had to do quite a lot of coaching with managers to get them to feel comfortable with the new model, as some feel the safety-net of the tick-box system has been removed. We have introduced role profiles which describe the 'how' and the 'what' and provide something against which managers and colleagues can be measured/assessed.

Paul Williams, Group HR Director at Smith & Nephew, emphasised the importance of good objective-setting in the performance management process:

It's not easy. Sometimes I think we focus too much on the important output elements – documentation, calibration etc, – to the detriment of the crucial input of quality objective setting. I also think we underestimate the skills and discipline needed to conceptualise and then communicate clear, meaningful and fully aligned objectives. Let's face it, we can develop the most sophisticated reviewing process but if the basic objectives are not well focused, then the outcome will be counterproductive. There's a great book sitting on my desk written by Bill Reddin in 1971 called Effective MBO. *It deals specifically with the issue of how to ensure that objectives are properly aligned, both vertically and horizontally. It also warns how HR people can 'freeze' the organisation by ignoring this. I used to have two copies of the book but a colleague sensibly stole one.*

Achieving line management buy-in

Approaches that can be adopted to achieve buy-in include:

- leadership from the top – conveying the message that performance management is an integral part of the fabric of the managerial practices of the organisation. This spells out the belief that this is what good management is about

- the involvement of line managers in the design and development of performance management processes as members of project teams or by taking part in pilot studies. This could be extended by the use of focus groups and, ideally, general surveys of opinions and reactions

- the inclusion of the ability to manage performance as a key criterion in assessing performance

- the use of 360-degree feedback to assess the performance management abilities of line managers when dealing with their staff and to indicate on an individual basis where improvements are required. If a full 360-degree system is not in use, then individuals can be asked specifically to assess how well their managers carried out their performance management responsibilities

- the conduct of regular surveys of the reactions of employees to performance management, leading to the identification of any weaknesses and the remedial action required

- systematic formal training in the performance management skills managers need to use. This should take place when launching a new scheme but, importantly, it should be built into management development programmes, especially for potential managers. It should be understood by them from the outset that performance management is an important part of their responsibilities, that these are the skills they must acquire and use, and that their performance will be measured by reference to the extent to which they are used effectively

- coaching and guidance for individual managers to supplement formal training. This can be provided by HR specialists, although ideally, experienced, committed and competent line managers can be used as coaches and mentors

- HR operating as a business partner alongside line managers so that they appreciate the significance of performance management to them and their staff.

An HR director at a financial services organisation informed us that training and emphasising development competencies are important:

We spent a lot of time training and developing managers to manage performance. We put everybody through a coaching programme, using the competency frameworks, and actively encourage the behaviours we have identified.

One of the competencies in the competency framework is about developing others, so therefore as a manager they would be assessed on that particular competency against their ability to develop the rest of their team.

It's difficult to put in place an objective that you will develop your staff, but because it was assessed and was one of the key competencies for every line manager it was demonstrably a key part of the management role. Obviously, some people were much better at it than others, so it would therefore form part of an individual development plan. For instance, they may need to get a better understanding of how to manage performance which is falling below expectations, or they may need to be more effective about the way they identify the training needs or put together the personal development plans.

My view is that at the end of the day, the performance appraisal process will only be as good as the managers delivering it, and some people are a lot better than others. But you can supply them with some tools to help,

Julie Hill, HR Partner, Retail Sales, Retail Development and HEA Central Sites, HBOS, described their HR partnership model:

The HR model in Halifax BOS is now one of working in partnership with the business. We go out into the business and see how the managers operate. We pick up issues with people at team meetings and management team meetings. We can then sit down and appreciate where there might be some problems that aren't being tackled.

At First Direct the emphasis is also on the business partner role of HR. As Jane Hanson, Organisation Development Manager, explained to us:

> *A business partner role for HR is very much a conduit of information. I attend all the senior managers' meetings at least monthly, often fortnightly or weekly, and we talk to them about what is coming up (for example, in performance management) and tell them what it's likely to look like. So we get buy-in from them.*

THE ETHICS OF PERFORMANCE MANAGEMENT

Four ethical principles which should be built into the performance management process have been proposed by Winstanley and Stuart-Smith.[20] These are: respect for the individual, mutual respect, procedural fairness, and transparency of decision-making.

The factors that affect perceptions of procedural justice as identified by Tyler and Bies[21] are: adequate consideration of an employee's viewpoint, suppression of personal bias towards an employee, applying criteria consistently across employees, providing early feedback to employees about the outcome of decisions, and providing employees with an adequate explanation of decisions made.

DEVELOPMENTS IN PERFORMANCE MANAGEMENT

The survey on which this book is based confirmed that the developments noted in the IPD 1997 survey[8] have been consolidated into good practice today. These can be summarised by the words used by our case study organisations:

- 'We expect managers who lead this organisation to behave in line with the stated core values. So the competencies reflect the values, and the individual performance management assessments are invited to assess how far managers are behaving in line with core values' – *Centrica*.

- 'We expect line managers to recognise it [performance management] as a useful contribution to the management of their teams rather than a chore' – *Centrica*.

- 'The principles behind performance management are career management and better performance' – *Cranfield University*.

- 'Making the management of performance an organic part of everyday life is not a series of mechanical tasks and processes' – *Halifax BOS*.

- 'Managing performance is about coaching, guiding, motivating and rewarding colleagues to help unleash potential and improve organisational performance. Where it works well it is built on excellent leadership and high-quality coaching relationships between managers and teams' – *Halifax BOS*.

- 'Performance management is designed to ensure that what we do is guided by our values and is relevant to the purposes of the organisation' – *Scottish Parliament*.

Endnotes

1 Hendry, C., Bradley, P. and Perkins, S. (1997) 'Missed'. *People Management*, 15 May, pp.20–5.

2 Lockett, J. (1992) *Effective Performance Management: A strategic guide to getting the best out of people*. London, Kogan Page.

3 Mohrman, A. M. and Mohrman, S. A. (1995) 'Performance management is "running the business"', *Compensation and Benefits Review*, July–August, pp.69–75.

4 Walters, M. (1995) *The Performance Management Handbook*. London, Institute of Personnel and Development.

5 Beer, M. and Ruh, R. A. (1976) 'Employee growth through performance management', *Harvard Business Review*, July–August, pp.59–66.

6 Institute of Personnel Management (1992) *Performance Management in the UK: an analysis of the issues*. London, IPM.

7 Bevan, S. and Thompson, M. (1991) 'Performance management at the crossroads', *Personnel Management*, November, pp.36–9.

8 Armstrong, M. and Baron, A. (1998) *Performance Management: The new realities*. London, CIPD.

9 Purcell, J., Kinnie, K., Hutchinson S., Rayton, B. and Swart, J. (2003) *Understanding the People and Performance Link: Unlocking the black box*. London, CIPD.

10 Boxall, P. (1996) 'The strategic HRM debate and the resource-based view of the firm', *Human Resource Management Journal*, 6(3), pp.59–75.

11 Kamoche, K. (1996) 'Strategic human resource management within a resource capability view of the firm', *Journal of Management Studies*, 33(2), pp.213–33.

12 Egan, G. (1995) 'A clear path to peak performance', *People Management*, 18 May, pp.34–7.

13 Incomes Data Services (1997) *Performance Management*. IDS Study No. 626. London, IDS.

14 Deming, W. E. (1986) *Out of the Crisis*. Cambridge, Mass., Massachusetts Institute of Technology, Center for Advanced Engineering Studies.

15 Ichniowski, C., Shaw, K. and Prennushi, G. (1997) 'The effects of human resource management practices on productivity: a study of steel finishing lines', *The American Economic Review*, June, pp.104–22.

16 Delery, J. E. and Doty, H. D. (1996) 'Modes of theorizing in strategic human resource management: tests of universality, contingency and configurational performance predictions', *International Journal of Human Resource Management*, 6, pp.656–70.

17 Huselid, M. A. (1995) 'The impact of human resource management: an agenda for the 1990s', *The International Journal of Human Resource Management*, 1(1), pp.17–43.

18 Guest, D. E. (1997) 'Human resource management and performance: a review of the research agenda', *The International Journal of Human Resource Management*, 8(3), pp.263–76.

19 Hutchinson, S. and Purcell, J. (2003) *Bringing Policies to Life – the vital role of front line managers*. London, CIPD.

20 Winstanley, D. and Stuart-Smith, K. (1996) 'Policing performance: the ethics of performance management', *Personnel Review*, Vol. 25 No. 6, pp.66–84.

21 Tyler, T. R. and Bies, R. J. (1990) 'Beyond formal procedures: the impersonal context of procedural justice', in J. S. Carroll (ed.), *Applied Social Psychology and Organizational Settings*. Hillsdale, N. J., Lawrence Earlbaum.

2

Performance management processes

Performance management was modelled in the last chapter as a cycle but in practice consists of a number of interconnected but not necessarily successive processes which take place throughout the year and which overlap. For example, although performance review and performance planning are identified correctly as separate activities, they may take place at the same time; a review of past performance referenced to a role profile will lead directly to plans for the future, also linked to a role profile. A performance review is not a separate activity taking place at an annual or twice-yearly meeting; it is, or should be, a continuous process so that the methods used in a formal review meeting are also used in informal reviews throughout the year.

Performance management processes are largely concerned with interactions between the parties involved, but they also relate to what individuals do about monitoring and improving their own performance, measuring performance, and documenting the outcomes of performance management plans and reviews. The processes are described in this chapter under the following headings:

- performance planning
- defining expectations
- objectives
- measuring performance
- the continuing process of performance management
- reviewing performance
- providing feedback
- assessing performance
- rating performance
- an alternative visual approach to rating
- coaching
- documentation.

Each of these refers to individual performance management. Managing organisational and team performance is examined in Chapter 9.

PERFORMANCE PLANNING

Performance planning is concerned with setting the direction, concluding performance agreements and agreeing personal development plans. It covers what has to be done, how it is done, and what is to be achieved. It is forward-looking, focusing on what people have to do to achieve their potential, and stretching them to discover what they are capable of. It also motivates people by giving them the opportunity to perform and develop and by recognising their achievements. But it is equally concerned with developing people – helping them to learn – and providing them with the support they need to do well, now and in the future.

Setting the direction

The direction is set by a plan based on the joint exploration of what individuals are expected to do and know, and how they are expected to behave to meet the requirements of their role and develop their skills and competencies. Expectations are agreed in terms of the results to be achieved and the improvements in competence and performance required. The plan also deals with how managers will provide the support and guidance individuals need. The process is forward-looking, although an analysis of performance in the immediate past may provide guidance on areas for improvement or development. This leads to the performance agreement which is the starting-point of the performance management cycle.

The performance agreement

The performance agreement that emerges from the planning process is based on the joint discussion and agreement of expectations (the process is described in the next section of this chapter). Performance agreements emerge from performance reviews. An assessment of past performance leads to an analysis of future requirements. The two processes can take place at the same meeting. Performance agreements are also influenced by organisational plans or strategies which result in cascading goals or objectives to be translated into individual objectives or actions.

Performance agreements record the agreed direction and form the basis for measurement, feedback, assessment and development in the performance management process. They define expectations – the results to be achieved and the skills, knowledge and expertise required to attain these results. Agreement is reached at this stage on the basis upon which performance will be measured and the evidence that will be used to establish levels of competence. It is important that these measures and evidence requirements should be identified and fully agreed now because they will be used jointly by managers and individuals and collectively by teams to monitor progress and demonstrate achievements.

Personal development planning

The performance planning stage includes the preparation and agreement of a personal development plan. This is an action plan for individuals to implement with the support of their managers and the organisation. It may include formal training but, more importantly, it will incorporate a wider set of development activities such as self-managed learning, coaching, project work, and job enlargement and enrichment. If multi-source assessment (360-degree feedback) is practised in the organisation, it will be used to identify development needs.

The development plan records the actions agreed to improve performance and to develop knowledge, skills and competencies. It is likely to focus on development in the current job – to improve the ability to perform it well and also, importantly, to enable individuals to take on wider responsibilities, extending their capacity to undertake a broader role. This plan therefore contributes to the achievement of a policy of continuous development which is based on the belief that everyone is capable of learning more and doing better in their jobs. But the plan will also contribute to enhancing the potential of individuals to carry out higher-level jobs. Personal development planning is discussed in more detail in Chapter 6.

DEFINING EXPECTATIONS

Performance management is largely about managing expectations. These are defined and agreed in the form of role profiles which set out what are in effect on-going objectives in the shape of definitions of what is required in each major aspect of the role. Expectations are also defined as short- to medium-term targets, the extension of knowledge and skills, upholding the core values of the organisation and meeting behavioural requirements. All these can be loosely referred to as objectives, which are more than simply output targets, as is often assumed. At Halifax Bank of Scotland the approach to describing the role and agreeing individual expectations is described thus:

Why? So colleagues have a clear picture of what is expected of them and how to achieve it.

When? Around the start of the year, and reviewed to reflect organisational and individual changes – eg business objectives, role changes, development needs.

How? Discussion between the individual and line manager to agree expectations across the full range of the job (ie business performance and personal style).

What? Identify the expectations of the role using role profiles, individual job descriptions, local business objectives:

- Consider the individual's performance in relation to this.
- Identify/agree areas for improvement.
- Get it documented by the individual and confirmed with the line manager.
- Discuss how the performance requirements will be delivered, supported and reviewed.

OBJECTIVES

The basis for managing expectations is an agreement between a manager and the individual on the latter's objectives and how achieving them will be measured. This informs performance planning, the management of performance throughout the year and the performance review. Objectives can be quantitative (numerical targets), achievement-based (things to be done), or qualitative (expectations of behaviour). Objectives can be work-related, referring to the achievement of role requirements (results to be attained). They can also be personal, taking the form of developmental or learning objectives which are concerned with what individuals should do to enhance their knowledge, skills and potential and to improve their performance or change their behaviour in specified areas.

Types of objectives

The various types of objectives are described below.

On-going role objectives

These are objectives which are built into roles. They are defined in role profiles as key result areas. For example, one of the key result areas for a sales representative could be: 'Respond to customer queries and complaints quickly in order to build customer satisfaction.' These objectives provide the basis for reviewing and assessing performance. Although described as on-going, they need to be reviewed regularly and can be modified accordingly.

Targets

Targets are quantifiable results to be attained which can be measured in such terms as output, throughput, income, sales, levels of service delivery, cost reduction, and reduction of reject rates. Thus a customer service target could be to respond to 90 per cent of queries within two working days.

Tasks/projects

Objectives can be set for the completion of tasks or projects by a specified date or to achieve an interim result.

Values

Expectations can be defined for upholding the core values of the organisation in such areas as quality, customer service, innovation, teamwork, care and consideration for people, environmental concern, and equal opportunities. The aim is to get people to 'live the values', ensuring that espoused values become values in use.

Behaviour

Behavioural expectations are often set out generally in competency frameworks, but they may also be defined individually under the framework headings. Competency frameworks may deal with areas of behaviour associated with core values – for example, teamwork – but they often convert the aspirations contained in value statements into more specific examples of desirable and undesirable behaviour which can help in planning and reviewing performance.

Performance improvement

Performance improvement objectives define what needs to be done to achieve better results.

Developmental

Developmental objectives specify areas for personal development in the shape of enhanced knowledge and skills (abilities and competencies).

What is a good objective?

Good work or operational objectives are:

- *consistent* with the values of the organisation and departmental and organisational objectives

- *precise* – clear and well-defined, using positive words

- *challenging* – to stimulate high standards of performance and to encourage progress

- *measurable* – they can be related to quantified or qualitative performance measures

- *achievable* within the capabilities of the individual – account should be taken of any constraints that might affect the individual's capacity to achieve the objectives; these could include lack of resources (money, time, equipment, support from other people), lack of experience or training, external factors beyond the individual's control, etc

- *agreed* by the manager and the individual concerned – the aim is to provide for the ownership, not the imposition, of objectives, although there may be situations where individuals have to be persuaded to accept a higher standard than they believe themselves to be capable of attaining

- *time-related* – achievable within a defined timescale (this would not be applicable to a standing or continuing objective)

- *focused on teamwork* – emphasising the need to work as an effective member of a team as well as stressing individual achievement.

Many organisations use the 'SMART' mnemonic to summarise the characteristics of good objectives:

Specific/stretching – clear, unambiguous, straightforward, understandable and

challenging

Measurable – quantity, quality, time, money

Achievable – challenging but within the reach of a competent and committed person

Relevant – relevant to the objectives of the organisation so that the goal of the individual is aligned to corporate goals

Time-framed – to be completed within an agreed timescale.

The process of defining expectations in the form of objectives

The definition of expectations should be based on a role profile which sets out the overall purpose of the role and the key result areas it contains. Role profiles should also define the competencies (knowledge and skills) required to achieve the role objectives and any particular behavioural requirements under the headings of the organisation's competency framework.

The process therefore starts at the performance planning stage by reviewing and as necessary amending the role profile, if one already exists, or creating a new role profile. In each of the key result areas the on-going role expectations and any specific targets or tasks, behavioural changes or development/training requirements related to those areas are discussed and agreed. In the example given earlier, the key result area might be amended to 'Respond to customer queries and complaints promptly, efficiently and politely in order to build customer satisfaction,' and the target could be redefined as 'Respond to 90 per cent of queries within one working day.' These expectations could be linked to a general discussion on how the individual could contribute to upholding a core value for customer service. An agreement could be reached by reference to the competency framework on any changes in behaviour required and how they can be achieved. The need for further training might also be identified and the discussion might end with a further agreement on how performance improvement in this area could be measured and assessed. This is an essential but difficult part of the process and it is necessary to agree either quantifiable performance measures or the type of evidence that can be made available to demonstrate that a job has been well done.

Setting objectives at Centrica

Joe Dugdale, HR Director, Centrica Telecommunications, told us that:

> *One of the things we are trying to do is strengthen the link between individual performance and business performance and make sure that the objectives and targets for individuals are aligned with the objectives of the organisation. For the most senior managers the intention is to have a direct alignment between the individual's objectives and his or her business unit's Management Agenda. We have seven major initiatives on our Management Agenda and we collectively check that individual objectives link back to them. If they don't, we tell the individual it is probably not the right objective. Objectives are then converted into key performance indicators so you can identify who is accountable for the delivery of particular services.*

MEASURING PERFORMANCE

To improve performance you have to know what current performance is. Indeed, it is often said that 'If you can't measure it, you can't manage it.' At the planning stage it is necessary to reach agreement on the criteria that will be used to assess the extent to which objectives have been achieved. These could be straightforward performance measures or metrics referring to quantified outputs. Or they could be equally clear performance indicators which refer to a task or project being completed which meets specified requirements. Such measures are relatively easy.

It becomes more difficult when qualitative measures have to be used which may refer to behaviours or unquantifiable outcomes rather than defined results. Performance assessments can then become much more judgemental and therefore potentially biased, unfair or inconsistent unless they are based on objective evidence of behaviour and the outcomes of behaviour. It is necessary to ensure that factual evidence is available on which to base judgements. In the example of the sales representative given above, evidence could be obtained to indicate performance levels with regard to promptness (computer records of speed of response), efficiency (records of follow-up queries or complaints from customers) and politeness (customer satisfaction surveys). The problem is that what gets measured is often what is easy to measure. And in some jobs what is meaningful is not measurable and what is measurable is not meaningful. As Levinson[1] pointed out:

The greater the emphasis on measurement and quantification, the more likely the subtle, non-measurable elements of the task will be sacrificed. Quality of performance frequently, therefore, loses out to quantification.

The classification of performance measures

Performance measures or metrics can be classified under a number of headings:

- *Finance* – income, shareholder value, added value, rates of return, costs
- *Output* – units produced or processed, throughput, sales, new accounts
- *Impact* – attainment of a standard (quality, level of service, etc), changes in behaviour, completion of work/project, level of take-up of a service, innovation
- *Reaction* – judgement by others: colleagues, internal and external customers
- *Time* – speed of response or turnaround, achievements compared with timetables, amount of backlog, time to market, delivery times.

Andy Neeley and Chris Adams[2] identify five distinct but interlocking perspectives of performance which can guide measurement:

1   stakeholder satisfaction – who are the key stakeholders, and what do they want and need?

2   strategies – what strategies do we have to put in place to satisfy the wants and needs of these key stakeholders?

3   processes – what critical processes do we require if we are to execute these strategies?

4   capability – what capabilities do we need to operate and enhance these processes?

5   stakeholder contribution – what contributions do we require from our stakeholders if we are to maintain and develop these capabilities?

Guidelines

Guidelines for defining performance measures comprise:

- Measures should relate to results and observable behaviours.
- Where appropriate, measures should be related to organisational measures of performance such as the balanced scorecard (see Chapter 8).
- The results should be within the control of the individual and based on agreed targets.
- Behavioural requirements (competencies) should be defined and agreed.
- Data (evidence) should be available for measurement.
- Measures should be objective.

Measuring performance is relatively easy for those who are responsible for achieving quantified targets – for example, sales. It is more difficult in the case of knowledge workers – for example, scientists. At the Institute of Cancer Research Neil Walford, Training and Organisational Development Manager, explained to us that:

It's difficult to manage scientific performance. In this field a breakthrough may suddenly come which changes everything, or nothing concrete will be achieved for two or three years. So it's quite hard when dealing with original research to quote specific measures and targets unless we use scientific measures that the researchers recognise. For our scientific staff we found that our performance reviews existed in their own little world and didn't have a great deal to do with their job. So you might get all the boxes ticked in performance review but your peers or managers might not necessarily think you were great.

We have therefore had to try to link scientific performance in with the strategy of the organisation. The role of the organisation is to set the context, put the resources in and generally assume that what scientists do fits with what we want. Someone described it as a scientist's hotel rather than a corporate structure. We create an environment where scientists come in and do their work, and this is heavily linked with the outside world ...

We try to identify the core values that make good scientists. If we can't get a hold on what performance is, we can't measure it, we can't replicate it. It's just trying to get a feel for what good science looks like.

Measurement in the case of scientists and possibly academics has to be qualitative, often concerned more with their overall contribution to achieving the aims of the organisation than setting specific targets and measuring performance against them. One method of dealing with this situation is to focus on behaviours (inputs) rather than the achievement of targets (outputs).

THE CONTINUING PROCESS OF PERFORMANCE MANAGEMENT

The aim should be to achieve 'performance management throughout the year' – it should be a continuous process. Performance management is not a once-a-year event. Conventional performance appraisal systems were usually built around an annual formal review, which tended to dwell on the past. This was carried out at the behest of personnel, often perfunctorily, and then forgotten. Boxes were ticked and the forms buried in the personnel department never to be seen or used again.

A formal, often annual, review is still an important part of a performance management framework but it is not the most important part. Equal, if not more, prominence is given to the performance agreement and the on-going practice of performance management.

Performance management should be regarded as an integral part of the continuing process of management. This is based on a philosophy which emphasises:

- the achievement of sustained improvements in performance

- the continuous development of skills and capabilities

- that the organisation is a 'learning organisation' in the sense that it is constantly developing and applying the learning gained from experience and the analysis of the factors that have produced high levels of performance.

Managers and individuals should therefore be ready, willing and able to define and meet development and improvement needs as they arise. As far as practicable, learning and work should be integrated. This means that encouragement should be given to all managers and members of staff to learn from the successes, challenges and problems inherent in their day-to-day work.

The process of continuing assessment should be carried out by reference to agreed objectives and to work, development and improvement plans. Progress reviews can take place informally. But there should be more formal interim reviews at, say, six months after the formal meeting. In some cases these points could be related to 'milestones' contained in project and work plans. Throughout the year, but especially during interim reviews, role profiles and objectives should be revised as circumstances change.

REVIEWING PERFORMANCE

Although performance management is a continuous process, it is still necessary to have a formal review once or twice yearly. This provides a focal point for the consideration of key motivational, performance and development issues. It is a means for considering the future in the light of an understanding of the past and present and answers the two fundamental questions of 'Where have we got to?' and 'Where are we going?' Reviews give managers and the individual members of their teams the opportunity to pause after the hurly-burly of everyday life and reflect on the key issues of personal development and performance improvement. They enable dialogues involving two-way communication on issues concerning work to take place, and this provides the basis for future work and development plans. Formal reviews do not replace informal or interim progress reviews but they can complement and enhance them, and therefore have an important part to play in performance management. In a sense, they are stocktaking exercises which take note of what has been happening in order to plan what is going to happen. A formal review is also necessary if performance has to be rated for contribution-related pay purposes.

The objectives of performance reviews

The objectives of performance reviews are:

- *motivation* – to provide positive feedback, recognition, praise and opportunities for growth; to clarify expectations; to empower people by encouraging them to take control over their own performance and development

- *development* – to provide a basis for developing and broadening abilities relevant both to the current role and any future role the individual may have the potential to carry out. Note that development can be focused on the current role, enabling people to enlarge and enrich the range of their responsibilities and the skills they require and be rewarded accordingly. This aspect of role development is even more important in flatter organisations where career ladders have shortened and where lateral progression is likely to be the best route forward

- *communication* – to serve as a two-way channel for communication about roles, expectations, relationships, work problems and aspirations.

Reviews can also provide the basis for rating performance, especially when ratings are required to inform contingent (performance-related or contribution-related) pay decisions. (Approaches to rating are examined later in this chapter.)

Conducting a performance review meeting

The performance review meeting should consist of a dialogue between the two people involved. It should take the form of a conversation, but a conversation with a purpose: to reach agreement on what has been achieved and what needs to be done in the future. The more informal the review the better.

The ten golden rules for conducting performance review meetings are:

1 *Be prepared*
Managers should prepare by referring to a list of agreed objectives and their notes on performance throughout the year. They should form views about the reasons for success or failure and decide where to give praise, which performance problems should be mentioned and what steps might be undertaken to overcome them. Thought should also be given to any changes that have taken place or are contemplated in the individual's roles, and to work and personal objectives for the next period.
Individuals should also prepare in order to identify achievements and problems, and to be ready to assess their own performance at the meeting. They should note any points they wish to raise about their work and prospects.

2 *Create the right atmosphere*
A successful meeting depends on creating an informal environment in which a full, frank but friendly exchange of views can take place. It is best to start with a fairly general discussion before getting into any detail.

3 *Work to a clear structure*
The meeting should be planned to cover all the points identified during preparation. But time should be allowed for individuals to express their views fully.

4 *Use positive feedback*
The review meeting provides a good opportunity for motivating people by recognising their achievements. Where possible, reviewers should begin with praise for some specific achievement, but this should be sincere and deserved. Praise helps people to relax – everyone needs encouragement and appreciation (approaches to feedback are discussed in the next section of this chapter).

5 *Let the individuals do most of the talking*
This enables them to get things off their chests and helps them to feel that they are getting a fair hearing. Use open-ended questions (ie questions that invite the individual to think about what to reply rather than indicating the expected answer). The aim is to encourage people to be expansive.

6 *Invite self-appraisal*
This is to see how things look from the individual's point of view and to provide a basis for discussion – many people underestimate themselves. Ask such questions as:
How well do you feel you have done?
What do you feel are your strengths?
What do you like most/least about your job?
Why do you think that project went well?
Why do you think you didn't meet that target?

7 *Discuss performance, not personality*
Discussions on performance should be based on factual evidence, not opinion. Always refer to actual events or behaviour and to results compared with agreed performance measures. Individuals should be given plenty of scope to explain why something did or did not happen.

8 *Encourage analysis of performance*
Do not just hand out praise or blame. Analyse jointly and objectively why things went well or badly and what can be done to maintain a high standard or to avoid problems in the future.

9 *Don't deliver unexpected criticisms*
There should be no surprises. The discussion should be concerned only with events or behaviours that have been noted at the time they took place. Feedback on performance should be immediate. It should not wait until the end of the year. The purpose of the formal review is to reflect briefly on experiences during the review period and on this basis to look ahead.

10 *Agree measurable objectives and a plan of action*
The aim should be to end the review meeting on a positive note.

PROVIDING FEEDBACK

Feedback is an important performance management process. It provides an opportunity to recognise achievements or to indicate areas for improvement or development. Feedback is always based on evidence. It refers to results, events, critical incidents and significant behaviours that have affected performance in specific ways. The feedback should be based on fact, not opinion, and should be presented in a way that enables individuals to recognise and accept its factual nature. Of course there will often be room for some interpretation of the facts, but such interpretations should start from the actual situation as reported in the feedback, not from the subjective views expressed by the provider of the feedback.

Guidelines on providing feedback

Provide feedback on actual events

Feedback should be provided on actual results or observed behaviour. It should be backed up by evidence. It should not be based on supposition about the reason for the behaviour. You might, for example, say: 'We have received a complaint from a customer that you have been uncooperative. Would you like to comment on this?', rather than: 'You tend to be aggressive.'

Provide immediate feedback

Do not wait until the review meeting to provide feedback. It should be given as soon as possible after the event so that it makes the most impact.

Describe, don't judge

The feedback should be presented as a description of what has happened – it should not be accompanied by a judgement. If you start by saying 'I have been informed that you have been rude to one of our customers. We can't tolerate that sort of behaviour,' you will instantly create resistance and prejudice an opportunity to encourage improvement.

Refer to specific behaviours

Relate all your feedback to specific items of behaviour. Do not indulge in transmitting general feelings or impressions.

Ask questions

Ask questions rather than make statements: 'Why do you think this happened?', 'On reflection, is there any other way in which you think you could have handled the situation?', 'How do you think you should tackle this sort of situation in the future?'

Select key issues

Select key issues and restrict yourself to them. There is a limit to how much criticism anyone can take. If you overdo it, the shutters will go up and you will get nowhere.

Focus

Focus on aspects of performance the individual can improve. It is a waste of time to concentrate on areas which the individual can do little or nothing about.

Provide positive feedback

Provide feedback on the things that the individual did well in addition to areas for improvement. People are more likely to work positively at improving their performance and developing their skills if they feel empowered by the process.

Build feedback into the job

As far as possible feedback should be built into the job – individuals should be given the opportunity and encouragement to measure their own performance.

ASSESSING PERFORMANCE

The assessment of performance in traditional performance appraisal schemes is based on the philosophy of management by objectives which involves clarifying with managers the key results and performance standards they must achieve and using systematic performance reviews to measure and discuss progress towards results by reference to the objectives. The major development in performance management over the last decade has been a concern with means and not just ends. This has arisen for the simple reason that performance development and improvement is only possible on the basis of an understanding not only of *what* has been done but also *how* it has been done.

The assessment of performance starts with a retrospective analysis of results and the reasons for the level of achievement reached. Results are assessed against agreed objectives. The analysis of reasons covers contextual (systems) considerations to answer the question 'Could the results be explained by the existence of factors beyond the individual's control?' The analysis can then continue to explore any individual behavioural factors that might have influenced performance. This behavioural analysis is best conducted by reference to a competency framework supported by evidence – examples of actual behaviour as agreed by the manager and the individual which contribute to good or not so good performance. An example of a framework developed for this purpose in a large housing association is given in Appendix A. This describes the types of behaviour under various headings expected at each of the six organisational levels.

The approach used in the Scottish Parliament is:

- The system involves measuring not only *whether* jobs are done but *how* they are done.

- Staff are assessed against a set of eight core areas of competence: (1) high-quality service, (2) flexibility and adaptability, (3) personal contribution, (4) problem-solving and decision-making, (5) leadership/teamwork, (6) communication and interpersonal skills, (7) parliamentary awareness, (8) equal opportunities – improving access and promoting equality. The competency areas are aligned to the job evaluation scheme factors.

- Positive and negative indicators exist against each area of competence to illustrate the ways in which staff are expected to behave and the ways in which they are expected not to behave.

One of the issues associated with assessment is whether or not some form of rating system should be used. This is examined below.

RATING PERFORMANCE

Traditional performance appraisal schemes almost always included some form of overall rating of performance. There are arguments for the use of rating as a summary of the assessment and to inform performance-related or contribution-related pay decisions. But there are also powerful arguments against. The pros and cons of rating are set out below.

Arguments for rating

- It is useful to sum up judgements about people – who are the exceptional performers or under-performers and who are the reliable core performers – so that action can be taken (developmental or some form of non-financial reward). It can be argued that everyone who carries out a review sums up their opinion of people, so why not place it on record for the individual?

- You cannot have contingent pay without ratings. However, this is not actually the case – 52 per cent of the organisations with contingent pay (42 per cent of those who responded to the CIPD survey) do not include ratings as part of the performance management process.

- They give people something to strive for, along the lines of 'You have given me a "C" rating' – what have I got to do to get a "B" rating?'

- They can provide a basis for predicting potential on the assumption that people who perform well in the present are likely to go on doing so in the future; however, past performance is only a predictor of future performance when there is a connecting link – ie when there are elements of the present job that are also important in a higher-level job.

Arguments against rating

- They are largely subjective and it is difficult to achieve consistency between the ratings given by different managers.

- To sum up the total performance of a person with a single rating is a gross over-simplification of what may be a complex set of factors influencing that performance – to do this after a detailed discussion of strengths and weaknesses suggests that the rating will be a superficial and arbitrary judgement.

- The whole performance review meeting may be dominated by the fact that it will end with a rating, especially if that governs contingent pay increases. This will severely limit the forward-looking and developmental focus of the meeting which is all-important.

- It *may* be feasible to rate performance against clearly defined quantitative objectives but it becomes much more difficult to rate fairly and consistently when dealing with more qualitative aspects of performance. It is particularly invidious to attempt to rate competency levels because they tend to be generalised statements of behavioural expectations which cannot support precise ratings, even if evidence of actual behaviour is available (which for assessment purposes it must be).

- To make judgements about potential on the basis of an overall rating which masks dissimilarities between these elements is dangerous, although it must be accepted that poor overall performance should not be followed or rewarded by promotion.

- To label people as 'average' or 'below average', or whatever equivalent terms are used, is both demeaning and demotivating.

The arguments against rating are more powerful than the arguments in favour. We found that more and more organisations have turned against rating when we compared the proportion of organisations which used rating in 1992 (78 per cent) with the proportion in 2003 (59 per cent). For example, one of our interviewees told us that:

> *We used to have alphabetical rating, ABCDE. However, when we reviewed the feedback it told us that the appraisal rating did not really add value. It was saying to people: 'You have achieved all your objectives and done a really good job – that's a C rating.' To them that was a satisfactory rating, so they would then ask, 'If I have done so well, why am I marked only as satisfactory?'*

However, if overall ratings are to be included in a performance review procedure, three things must be considered:

- the basis upon which levels of performance are to be defined
- the number of rating levels to be used
- methods of achieving a reasonable degree of accuracy and consistency in ratings.

Performance-level definitions

The rating-scale format can either be behavioural with examples of good, average and inadequate performance, or graphic which simply presents a number of scale points along a continuum. The scale points or anchors in the latter may be defined alphabetically (a, b, c, etc), numerically (1, 2, 3, etc) or by means of abbreviations or acronyms (*ex* for 'excellent', etc) which purport to disguise the hierarchical nature of the scale. The scale points may be further described adjectivally (eg exceptional, acceptable, unsatisfactory).

The following is a typical example of a five-point rating scale which progresses downwards from highly positive to negative:

A Outstanding performance in all respects

B Superior performance, significantly above normal job requirements

C Good all-round performance that meets the normal requirements of the job

D Performance not fully up to requirements. Clear weaknesses requiring improvement have been identified

E Unacceptable – constant guidance is required and performance of many aspects of the job is well below a reasonable standard.

An alternative and increasingly popular approach is to have a rating scale such as the following four-point one, which provides positive reinforcement or at least emphasises development needs at every level.

Very effective   Consistently performs in a thoroughly proficient manner beyond normal expectations

Effective	**Achieves required objectives and standards of performance and meets the normal expectations of the job**
Developing	**A contribution that is stronger in some aspects of the job than others, where most objectives are met but where performance improvements should still take place**
Basic	**A contribution which indicates that there is considerable room for improvement in several definable areas.**

Note also that in order to dispel any unfortunate associations with other systems such as school reports, this 'positive' scale does not include alphabetic or numerical ratings.

Number of rating levels

The most common number of rating levels in those respondents to the CIPD survey who used them was four (28 per cent of respondents) and five (47 per cent of respondents). Three levels were used by 5 per cent of respondents. Traditionally, five-level scales have been used on the grounds that raters prefer this degree of fineness in performance definition and can easily recognise the middle grade and distinguish those who fall into higher or lower categories. Four-level scales are often used when it is believed that they avoid the problem inherent in five-level scales of rating drift (unwillingness to use the middle or lower categories). Three-level scales are advocated by some organisations because they believe that people are not capable of making any finer distinctions between performance levels. Managers know the really good and poor performers when they see them and have no difficulty in placing the majority where they belong – ie in the middle category.

The number of levels to use is a matter of choice and judgement but there is no evidence that any single approach is clearly superior to the others. It is, however, preferable for level definitions to be positive rather than negative and for them to provide a degree of reliable guidance on the choice of ratings.

Achieving consistency

The problem with rating scales is that it is difficult to ensure that a consistent approach is adopted by managers to rating throughout an organisation. There is plenty of room for subjective and biased judgements, and this creates difficulties when rating decisions are converted into contingent pay decisions. Performance-related pay schemes have often failed because the people affected do not trust their managers to be fair. The approaches that can be adopted to assist achieving consistency are:

1 *Forced distribution*
   This requires managers to conform to a pattern which quite often corresponds broadly with the normal curve of distribution. A typical distribution would be:

Rating %
A   5
B   15
C   60
D   15
E   5

But the distribution of ability between different departments may vary and managers rightly dislike being forced to conform to some arbitrary pattern. Only 8 per cent of the respondents to the CIPD survey used forced distribution.

2   *Ranking systems*
An alternative approach is to rank staff in order of merit and then the rank order is divided into segments that indicate ratings. A typical forced distribution in a ranking system would be to give the top 10 per cent an A rating, the next 15 per cent a B rating, the next 60 per cent a C rating and the remaining 15 per cent a D rating. Such distribution systems do ensure a consistent distribution of ratings but still depend on the relative objectivity and accuracy of the rankings.

3   *Training*
Training can take place in the form of 'consistency' workshops for managers who discuss how ratings can be objectively justified and test rating decisions on case study performance review data. This can build a level of common understanding about rating levels.

4   *Calibration (peer reviews)*
Groups of managers meet to review the pattern of each other's ratings and challenge unusual decisions or distributions. This process of calibration or moderation is time-consuming but is possibly the best way to achieve a reasonable degree of consistency, especially when the calibration group members share some knowledge of the performances of each other's staff. Manager workshops to review ratings were held by 16 per cent of the respondents to the 2003 survey.

5   *Monitoring*
The distribution of ratings is monitored by HR, which challenges any unusual patterns and identifies and questions what appear to be unwarrantable differences between departments' ratings. This is the approach favoured by many organisations, although there is much to be said for supporting it with training and peer reviews.

6   *Grandparenting*
This corresponds to a review of individual line managers' ratings by a more senior manager – usually their immediate superior – who checks for anomalies and unusual patterns. The system was used by 18 per cent of the respondents to the 2003 survey.

AN ALTERNATIVE VISUAL APPROACH TO RATING

An alternative approach to rating was developed by Ann Cummins of Humanus Consultancy for a client in the financial services sector. This involves agreement between the manager and the individual on where the latter should be placed on a matrix or grid as shown in Figure 3. This provides a 'snapshot' of their overall contribution, which is presented visually and may therefore provide a better basis for analysis and discussion than a mechanical rating. The assessment of contribution refers both to outputs and to behaviours, attitudes and overall approach.

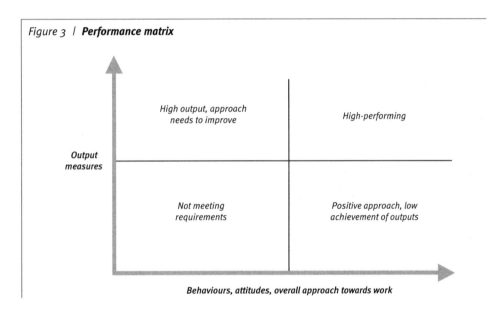

Figure 3 | **Performance matrix**

The review guidelines that accompany the matrix are:

You and your manager need to agree an overall assessment. This will be recorded in the summary page at the beginning of the review document. The aim is to get a balanced assessment of your contribution through the year. The assessment will take account of how you have performed against the responsibilities of your role as described in the role profile, the objectives achieved, and your competency development over the course of the year. The assessment will become relevant for pay increases in the future.

The grid on the annual performance review summary is meant to provide a visual snapshot of your overall contribution. This replaces a more conventional rating-scale approach. It reflects the fact that your contribution is determined not just by results but also by your overall approach towards your work and how you behave towards colleagues and customers.

The evidence recorded in the performance review will be used to support where your manager places a mark on the grid.

Your manager's assessment against the vertical axis will be based on an assessment of your performance against your objectives, the performance standards described in your role profile, and any other work achievements recorded in the review. Together these represent 'outputs'.

The assessment against the horizontal axis will be based on an overall assessment of your performance against the competency level definitions for the role.

Note that someone who is new in the role may be placed in one of the lower quadrants, but this should be regarded as an indication of development needs and not as a reflection on an individual's performance.

A similar 'matrix' approach has been adopted by Halifax BOS. It is used for management appraisals to illustrate their performance against peers. It is not an 'appraisal rating' – the purpose of the matrix is to help individuals focus on what they do well and also reveal any areas for improvement.

Two dimensions – business performance and behaviour (management style) – are reviewed on the matrix as illustrated in Figure 4 to ensure a rounder discussion of overall contribution against the full role demands rather than a short-term focus on current results.

This is achieved by visual means: the individual is located at the relevant position on the matrix by reference to the two dimensions. For example, a strong people

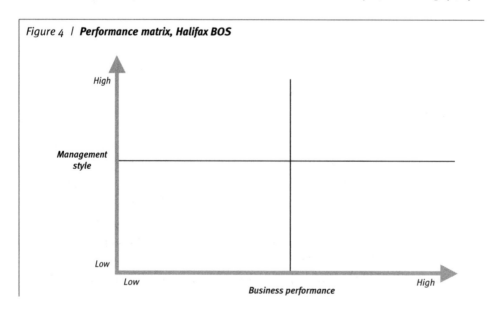

Figure 4 | *Performance matrix, Halifax BOS*

manager who is low on the deliverables would be located somewhere in the top left-hand quadrant, and the aim would then be movement to a position in the top right-hand quadrant.

COACHING

The improvement of performance that is the main aim of performance management is to a large extent the responsibility of the manager as coach, supporting people in their endeavours to develop their knowledge and skills. The need for coaching may arise from formal or informal performance reviews but opportunities for coaching will emerge during the normal day-to-day activities.

Every time a manager delegates a new task to someone, a coaching opportunity is created to help the individual learn any new skills or techniques that are needed to get the job done. Every time a manager provides an individual with feedback after a task has been completed, there is an opportunity to help that individual do better next time.

The coaching process

Coaching as part of the normal process of management consists of:

- making people aware of how well they are performing by, for example, asking them questions to establish the extent to which they have thought through what they are doing

- controlled delegation – ensuring that individuals not only know what is expected of them but also understand what they need to know and be able to do to complete the task satisfactorily. This gives managers an opportunity to provide guidance at the outset – guidance at a later stage may be seen as interference

- using whatever situations that arise as opportunities to promote learning

- encouraging people to look at higher-level problems and how they would tackle them.

Coaching skills

Coaching is most effective when:

- the coach understands that his or her role is to help people to learn

- individuals are motivated to learn – they should be aware that their present level of knowledge or skill or their behaviour has to be improved if they are going to perform their work to their own and to others' satisfaction

- individuals are given guidance on what they should be learning and feedback on how they are doing

- learning is an active, not a passive, process – individuals must be actively involved with their coach

- the coach listens to individuals to understand what they want and need

- the coach adopts a constructive approach, building on strengths and experience.

Examples

One of our interviewees in a financial services organsiation told us:

> *We tried to develop a coaching culture. We put people through a coaching programme to give them confidence in being coaches. Coaching doesn't mean that you have to sit down for an hour with someone – it might be a 30-second discussion with some feedback. We build it into the fabric of what we do. We encourage people to do it as part of the normal day-to-day routine. We have had to overcome the usual challenges – 'Well, how do I find time for all of this?' But we have stressed that that's part and parcel of the manager's role by putting it in as part of the competency framework. So managers have become much better coaches.*

At HBOS coaching is seen as part of everyday life. It is not paper-driven – the emphasis is on continuous dialogue between managers and individuals concerning performance and then acting accordingly.

DOCUMENTATION

Performance management is not a form-filling exercise, as many traditional merit-rating or performance appraisal schemes tended to be. But it is necessary to maintain records of amendments to role profiles and agreed objectives when reviewing performance throughout the year, and contingent pay schemes require a record of assessments or ratings. The main purpose of any performance management forms is to serve as working documents. Forms should record agreements on performance achievements and actions to be taken to improve performance or develop competence and skills. They should be dog-eared from much use – they should not be condemned to moulder away in a file.

When designing performance management forms the aim should be to keep them as simple and brief as possible while allowing ample 'white space' for comments. Like all good forms, they should be self-explanatory, but they may be supplemented by notes for guidance. The essential information to be recorded on a form should be:

- the key result areas from the role profile

- the objectives agreed for each key result area

- the values or competency headings

- the assessment of performance against each key result area and values or competency heading

- details of any plans for performance improvement and development.

An example of a form containing these details is given in Appendix B.

Data

The ability of organisations to communicate the value and contribution of people to key stakeholders in the business has now been recognised as extremely useful to a true understanding of the long-term potential performance of organisations. The financial world now recognises that a large part of organisational value is made up of intangible value much of which is about people.

However, because so-called human capital is more difficult to measure than other forms of capital it has often been neglected in management decision-making. Real efforts are now being made not just by HR people but also in the accountancy profession to develop frameworks and measures that give a true understanding of human capital value.

Performance management generates a great deal of performance data which if captured and analysed appropriately could contribute to a greater understanding of the value of people and their contribution and aid management decision-making. Some organisations are therefore developing different types of documentation such as so-called 'dashboards' or performance indicators into which they can feed data gleaned from the performance management process to inform managers and measurement frameworks. This aspect of performance management is examined in greater depth in Chapter 5.

Endnotes

1 Levinson, H. (1970) 'Management by whose objectives?', *Harvard Business Review*, July–August, pp.125–34.

2 Neeley, A. and Adams, C. (2002) 'The performance prism', *Encyclopaedia of Social Measurement*. Elsevier.

3

Performance management: comments and issues

critical evaluation

Performance management has attracted a lot of attention, mainly from academics. The aim of this chapter is to review the literature and draw conclusions from it to provide guidance for practitioners on the issues that have to be addressed in developing and applying performance management. The chapter starts with an analysis of the main issues raised by the commentators as summarised in the next section. Many of the academics and writers in this field have expressed a negative view of performance management based on the argument that it fails to achieve its purpose largely because its fails to recognise the complexity of the process. The chapter concludes with suggestions on the actions that can be taken by practitioners to respond to the messages delivered by the literature.

critically evaluate

PERFORMANCE MANAGEMENT ISSUES

The main issues concerning performance management as identified by writers and researchers are set out below and cross-referenced to the literature.

1 The problem of gaining the commitment of line managers to performance management and of getting to do it well, or at all (Carlton and Sloman; Englemann and Roesch; Furnham; Stiles *et al*)

2 The process is problematic because of the complexity and difficulties involved in one person's attempting to sum up the performance of another: 'Performance appraisal requires subtle psychological and social skills which may not be acquired by many managers' (Bowles and Coates)

3 The prevalence of poorly designed or poorly administered performance management schemes (Engelmann and Roesch)

4 The tendency of managements to adopt a unitary frame of reference ('We're all in it together, our interests coincide') when in reality organisations are more likely to be pluralistic in the sense that there are divergent interests that should be acknowledged (Newton and Findlay; Townley; Winstanley and Stuart-Smith)

5 Managements indulge in rhetoric about development but often do not put their espoused views into practice (Stiles *et al*)

6 Appraisal ignores system factors (Bowles and Coates; Deming)

7 Appraisal is an inconsistent and fundamentally subjective process (Grint)

8 Performance management is wrongly focused on financial rewards (Hendry, Woodward, Bradley and Perkins)

9 Performance management is a means of oppressive or coercive control (Barlow; Grint; Hendry; Newton and Findlay; Townley; Winstanley and Stuart-Smith)

10 Both line managers and employees tend to be disenchanted with performance management (Stiles, Gratton and Truss).

COMMENTS ON PERFORMANCE MANAGEMENT

G. Barlow (1989) 'Deficiencies and the perpetuation of power: latent functions in performance appraisal'[1]

Arguments

'Institutionally elaborated systems of management appraisal and development are significant rhetorics in the apparatus of bureaucratic control.' They reward what is perceived to be successful performance and penalise deviance.

Appraisal systems impose artificial rationality. 'Ambiguity and complexity will not be eliminated from the pluralistic processes and alliances of organisational life as it actually is.'

Evidence from field study in the petrochemicals industry

The study established from managers that the appraisal system 'served neither to motivate nor control'. Managers saw the appraisal system as a bureaucratic ritual. The system:

> institutionalised an ideology which sought to enlist participants' positive effort and continued compliance, despite the inegalitarian nature of business organisations.

Conclusion

The conclusion was that:

> The dynamic of power relationships is bound up with their intangibility ... Such relationships evolve from the myriad intangible observations and devices by means of which one person learns how to relate to and work with another. Formalised appraisal systems discount the influences of such dynamics because they cannot be enumerated satisfactorily. In doing so they ride roughshod over what frequently is precarious and tenuous.

M. Bowles and G. Coates (1993) 'Image and substance: the management of performance as rhetoric or reality?'[2]

Arguments

Appraisal is shifting from concern with performance to concern with people in terms of their identification with the job and the organisation. 'Believing in the organisation is the criterion, rather than performing for it.'

Managers are mostly appraised by results, but results alone cannot reflect performance as it is still affected by many other factors. Deming (1986) is right: job performance cannot be disentangled from systems effects.

The emphasis given to collective effort and teamwork conflicts with the individualistic ethic of performance appraisal practice.

The nature of performance appraisal, which involves one individual making judgements on another, 'tends to reinforce authority relations and defines dependency'.

Research

A survey of 48 organisations in the Midlands established that the major benefit claimed by those with what they considered to be successful systems was its use in getting people to achieve work goals. The problems faced by organisations experiencing some difficulties were measuring performance and the extra demands made on managers.

Conclusions

'Performance appraisal requires subtle psychological and social skills which may not be acquired by many managers.'

Performance appraisal seems to be often 'an opportunistic means to address performance issues', rather than 'a well thought out, coherent and systematic attempt to impart a new philosophy and practice of organisational relations'.

'The absence of clear indices of measurement will often cause images of performance to be exploited.' Performance may have less to do with physical outputs and more about exhibiting the correct mindset.

An ethic is required which 'conveys trust, integrity and faith in the ability of employees to contribute to a creative management practice'.

Management should provide the 'enabling' conditions through which work is performed.

'The active involvement of employees in the management of performance potentially allows a constructive dialogue with management, to determine what factors foster performance.'

Ian Carlton and Martyn Sloman (1992) 'Performance appraisal in practice'[3]

A review of the appraisal system in a merchant bank revealed the following problems:

- Managers were hostile to what they perceived as bureaucracy and disliked form-filling.

- Ratings linked to pay were disliked. As one line manager said: 'Performance appraisal is a load of rubbish. You decide on the rating you want to put in the box and then make up a few words of narrative in other sections to justify it.'

- Ratings drift occurred. Managers tended to over-rate people because of the link between appraisal and pay. As one manager commented when challenged: 'I knew that his performance did not justify the rating but I thought it would demotivate him if I marked him down.'

- The separation of appraisal and pay decisions was considered to be impossible because 'managers only fill in one form, and if they do not perceive a clear link with salary, they will not do it'.

William Deming (1986) *Out of the Crisis* [4]

In the twelfth of his fourteen points, Deming made the following pronouncement:

Remove the barriers that rob hourly workers and people in management of their right to pride in workmanship. This implies, inter alia, abolition of the annual merit rating (appraisal of performance).

He also defined 'evaluation of performance, merit rating or annual review' as the third deadly disease of management.

The further points he made were that:

- rating the performance of individuals is unsound because differences in performance are largely due to systems variations

- targets and objectives for individuals damage customer-focused teamwork

- targets too often make no reference to the customer and results are limited if 'stretching' can only be achieved by sub-optimisation, while, on the other hand, soft targets may be negotiated

- formal appraisal schemes reinforce managers' reluctance to engage in coaching and open, direct regular dialogue with people

- reliance on pay as a motivator destroys pride in work and individual creativity.

C. H. Engelmann and C. H. Roesch (1996) *Managing Individual Performance* [5]

Englemann and Roesch list the following negative consequences of poorly designed or poorly administered performance management schemes, or schemes that lack management commitment:

- poor motivation and self-esteem because employees receive inadequate feedback on their work performance
- little or no focused communication about performance between supervisors and employees
- inefficient use of supervisors' time
- litigation over alleged discriminatory actions.

Adrian Furnham (1996) 'Starved of feedback'[6]

Adrian Furnham made the following comment: 'The question is why this fundamental process [performance appraisal] is so rare, and when done at all, is frequently done badly.' He suggested the following reasons for this situation:

- Pusillanimity – managers are too scared to give negative or corrective feedback.
- Managers have not been trained in the skills of appraisal.
- Managers argue that rather than having a couple of specific hour-long meetings over the year, they give subordinates consistent feedback on a day-to-day basis. But what they fail to realise is that discussions about software, the sales figures and the strategic plan are not appraisal.
- The organisation, despite much rhetoric, does not take the whole process seriously.

Keith Grint (1993) 'What's wrong with performance appraisal? A critique and a suggestion'[7]

Dislike of appraisal systems

There seems to be considerable, although not universal, dislike and dissatisfaction with all performance appraisal systems to some degree. Crudely speaking, human resource managers seem favourably inclined, line managers much less so.

Problems with appraisals

The problems with appraisals are:

- the complexity of the variables being assessed
- the subjective elements that confuse the assessment
- the fact that rewards and progress are in the hands of a single 'superordinate' (ie appraiser/manager)
- the fact that individuals have to work with their appraisers after the appraisal
- the fundamental issue relating to the appraisal by individuals of individuals who only act in social situations – the comment is made that a major aim of appraisal schemes is to limit the collective aspects of work and

individualise the employment relationship. 'F. W. Taylor would indeed have been impressed.'

The unreal nature of assessments

The extent to which assessments bear a close or, indeed, any relationship to reality is questioned because:

- the assessor only sees the assessed from one specific position
- of the impossibility of 'being able to reduce the complex nature of any individual to a series of scales in a tick list'
- the multifaceted identity of people may lead to views about individuals varying widely – different people read each other very differently
- as people ascend the hierarchy they are likely to be less and less aware of what their subordinates think about them and their performance
- the possibility of ever achieving objective appraisals of a subordinate by a superior is remote.

Conclusions

'Rarely in the history of business can such a system have promised so much and delivered so little.' But in spite of the relatively long and generally unhappy life of appraisal schemes they should not be abandoned. Instead, they should be considered more sceptically – people might have to accept their 'subjective fate'.

Chris Hendry, Sally Woodward, Paola Bradley and Stephen Perkins (2000)[8]

These academics make the somewhat sweeping statement that 'In most organisations it [performance management] is conducted in a superficial way, and its significance to the HR role is not properly appreciated.' This assertion is not supported by any evidence.

They suggest that performance management is 'vitiated' by the motivation to control: 'Too often it is more about exercising control than contributing to real development.' Their focus is on what they term 'the dark side' of performance management which arises from inappropriate links to rewards. (Presumably they mean financial rewards – reward management, if properly conducted, provides plenty of opportunities for non-financial rewards such as recognition through feedback and the creation of opportunities for personal development.) In their view, employees may be financially motivated 'but are they motivated to do the things which contribute effectively to business strategy?'

They comment that problems with performance management are 'frequently put down to the deficiencies of the line manager, who is seen as the weak link in a system designed and imposed by others'. In this connection they observe, sensibly, that:

Performance management needs to be seen first and foremost as a management process. If it overloads the ordinary manager, makes his or her job more difficult and distracts from tasks which are more productive, it is failing.

Douglas McGregor (1957) 'An uneasy look at performance appraisal'[9]

One of the most powerful blasts against performance appraisal was delivered by Douglas McGregor as long ago as 1957 in his *Harvard Business Review* article 'An uneasy look at performance appraisal'. He attacked the top-down, backward-looking nature of appraisal. But in marked contrast to many other commentators on performance appraisal he did not content himself with destructive criticism. Instead, he produced a number of positive ideas which, even if they are not totally in line with current thinking, at least pointed to the way ahead. He suggested that the focus should be on the future rather than on the past and emphasised the need to shift from appraisal to analysis.

This implies a more positive approach. No longer is the subordinate being examined by the superior so his [sic] weaknesses may be determined; rather he is examining himself in order to define not only his weaknesses but also his strengths and potentials . . . He becomes an active agent, not a passive 'object' . . . There is less tendency for the personality of the subordinate to become an issue. The superior . . . can become a coach, helping the subordinate to reach his own decisions on the specific steps that will enable him to reach his targets.

In this respect, as in many others, McGregor pioneered what are now many of the accepted practices of human resource management.

Tim Newton and Patricia Findlay (1996) 'Playing God? The performance of appraisal'[10]

Arguments

Most writers on appraisal are over-influenced by the 'neo-human relations' writers of the 1950s and 1960s (eg Douglas McGregor), who provide 'unitarist prescriptions that are generally insensitive to both context and outcome' and assume that appraisal will serve the supposed common interest of employer and employee. (Clearly these academics have not read McGregor.)

Appraisees are not going to view appraisal as a 'helping/counselling exercise' if there is the possibility that the data will be used in assessing promotion or demotion.

Participative approaches to appraisal are suspect because they constitute 'a desire through which management control may be enhanced by appearing to disperse it'.

Appraisal can be regarded as a management strategy 'aimed at eliciting a measure of voluntary compliance from employees' and encouraging workers to regulate and police their own behaviour.

The 'neo-human relations' assumption that appraisal can equally serve the appraiser and the appraisee is rejected.

Conclusion

A greater understanding of the organisational context in which appraisal takes place and, consequently, of appraisal itself, requires an acknowledgement of the differences of interests between appraisers and appraisees.

Philip Stiles, Linda Gratton and Catherine Truss (1997) 'Performance management and the psychological contract'[11]

On the basis of their research, these academics from the London Business School raised the issue of linking performance to strategy. They noted that the three organisations they studied had introduced value statements and the aim was to derive individual objectives from the organisation strategy and values. But they also observed that:

> *The short-term demands of the business meant that in some cases the targets expressed in terms of corporate values (for example teamwork or innovation) were given low priority by managers who saw the real goal as satisfying budgetary or financial targets.*

Furthermore,

> *The objectives were generally set by the employee's boss, not as the result of a joint negotiation. The objectives therefore tended to be viewed as imposed, and there was a consequent difficulty in employees being motivated by them.*

Overall, they commented that 'despite the strong organisational emphasis given to the appraisal process, at the operating level there was a considerable degree of management apathy and even scepticism towards carrying out appraisal', and that 'the evidence suggests that employees are largely disenchanted' (in fact, no evidence was quoted for these assertions). The reasons stated for this were:

- the perceived bureaucracy of the appraisal process
- the lack of positive outcomes from the process
- variations between individual managers on judging performance
- the defensive use of appraisal (managers were content to rate people as average)
- appraisals were often too short to allow full discussion of an employee's contribution and outcomes.

Barbara Townley (1990/1991) 'Appraisal into UK universities'[12]

An analysis of 30 University appraisal schemes generated the following general comments on appraisal:

- Appraisal is regarded as a technical function which is considered in isolation.
- Appraisal should be viewed as 'an assemblage of signs whose meaning is construed dependent on the context of its introduction and operation'.

- A failure to contextualise appraisal will ignore the 'different, sometimes conflicting interests' which influence the form of appraisal adopted.

- Seeing appraisal in the context in which it operates 'points to the diversity of functions into which a single system may be invested'.

- Appraisal can become a 'mechanism around which interests are negotiated, counter-claims articulated and political processes expressed. Designers of appraisal schemes would do well to remember this.'

- A university is quoted as stating that 'the term "appraisal" usually implies a judgement by a superior of a subordinate, that is, a process which is unilateral and top-down.'

Barbara Townley (1990) 'A discriminating approach to appraisal'.[13]

Management is institutionally empowered to determine and/or regulate certain aspects of the actions of others. The concept of control is central to an understanding of management.

> *Power is exercised through its intersection with knowledge – for example, methods of observation, techniques of registration – mechanisms for the supervision and administration of individuals and groups.*

Appraisal is defined as a managerial activity – 'the provision of data designed to ensure that resources are used efficiently in accomplishing organisational objectives'. The role of appraisers is structured through setting the agenda. Management is inextricably linked to control over the labour process.

One of the inherent paradoxes of appraisal is that 'the information required to ensure effective work organisation will not be forthcoming if it is thought that this will jeopardise the individual'.

Appraisal operates as a form of 'panopticon' [a concept for prison design originated by Jeremy Bentham in the nineteenth century which incorporates a central observation tower from which the activities of all the inmates can be seen]. The process of appraisal takes this form because it combines hierarchy, unilateral observation and 'a normalising judgement'. Anonymous and continuous surveillance are methods of articulating a monitoring role.

Appraisal is the 'exercise of control at a distance both spatially and temporally'. It 'illustrates how knowledge of the individual and the work performed articulates the managerial role as a directional activity'.

Diana Winstanley and Kate Stuart-Smith (1996) 'Policing performance: the ethics of performance management'[14]

Argument

Traditional approaches to performance management fail because they are flawed in implementation, demotivate staff and 'are often perceived as forms of control which are inappropriately used to "police" performance'.

Criticisms of performance management

- lack of conclusive evidence that it leads to improved performance
- can produce undesirable side-effects: demotivation on the one hand and over-bureaucratisation on the other
- difficult to set performance objectives which cover intangibles, are flexible in response to change and cover the whole job
- lack of time given to the process
- in the perception of appraisees, can 'become akin to a police state' where evidence is collected, dossiers built up and 'supervision becomes a matter of spying through keyholes': it is a form of 'Taylorism'
- is managerialist in that it takes a unitary view of the organisation. This is referred to as the 'radical critique' of performance management – namely that 'it operates within a unitarist paradigm and is not able to treat organisations as pluralities of interests'
- begs the question: 'Are individuals in the process treated as ends in themselves or merely means to other ends?' (it is suggested that the latter approach is typical)
- reinforces modes of 'intrusive control'.

Ethical principles

Four ethical principles should be built into the performance management process:

- respect for the individual
- mutual respect
- procedural fairness
- transparency of decision-making.

Performance management model

The model used consists of three main processes:

- setting the objectives
- managing performance to the objectives
- measuring performance against the objectives.

Proposals

It is suggested that a stakeholder perspective should be adopted in the design of performance management systems which offers a wider role to individuals as 'creators' rather than 'victims' of performance management. Because pluralism is endemic in organisations, it should not only be the power-holder's voice that is heard: 'Where consensus exists, it can be built in, but where it does not, dissenters are not silenced.'

The approach should be one of 'stakeholder synthesis' which goes beyond the analysis of the interests of stakeholders to gaining their views about business strategy and incorporating these views in the system design.

The case study

The case study describes how 'multi-fiduciary stakeholder analysis' was used to develop performance management processes at the British School of Osteopathy. This included interviews with key stakeholders to agree strategic objectives for the organisation, the use of the 'Delphi technique' to obtain individual views that would not be dominated by those of other people, focus group meetings with tutors and customers (students), and questionnaires and depth interviews with customers (patients).

Conclusion

The focus must move away from measurement and judgement and towards 'developing understanding and building up trust to allow a genuine dialogue to take place'.

COMMENTS ON THE COMMENTARIES

The views expressed by the commentators provide a different perspective on performance management from that offered in more prescriptive books and articles. And it is an interesting perspective. It penetrates beyond the rhetoric (a favourite term of abuse employed by the academics) to the forces that are actually at work when performance management is operated. It has to be recognised that in many organisations (but not those we contacted) performance appraisal as used traditionally, *can* be no more than a means of enlisting compliance, as these writers assert. It is also possible that much appraisal is carried out badly, although this was not confirmed by our research. And when appraisal schemes involve top-down judgement, they *can* be instruments through which unilateral power is exercised. Moreover, there is a danger that the rhetoric of performance will not be converted to reality because it ultimately depends on the commitment and capability of line managers, and this cannot be guaranteed.

There *is* also a danger that performance management becomes bureaucratic, and if it includes performance ratings, these *can* be inconsistent and based on subjective opinions.

All these aspects of how performance management functions in organisations should be borne in mind when considering its introduction or amendment. When management says it wants to create 'shared understanding', does it really believe what is being said? And will something be done about the processes (including, for example, communication, training, support, guidance, counselling and evaluation) required to ensure that it happens? If not, the accusation of many academics that much of what is said about performance management is meaningless is justified. And if management says it believes in a stakeholder approach, will something be done about it which does recognise that the organisation is a community of interests, all of which will not necessarily coincide? The doubts expressed on the likelihood of that happening by the writers quoted in this chapter may well be justified in many organisations.

So there is much to be learned from these commentators. However, there is a reservation that can be made about them. They have mainly concentrated on performance appraisal as practised in the 1980s, when the failings they have identified were indeed rife. Our research indicates that the performance management process has moved on, and that people management practitioners have heeded the lessons of the past. For example, many of our interviewees stressed the role of the line manager in delivering performance management, and in many instances they did not feel able to enforce performance management. Rather, they sought to encourage line managers to use it by a process of education in the benefits to both them personally and the organisation.

Only 49 per cent of those with performance management who responded to the CIPD questionnaire used ratings. Performance appraisal in the crude judgemental sense was not therefore practised in the majority of organisations. This is a distinct step forward. And evidence from interviews and focus groups is that performance management processes are increasingly conforming to the Winstanley and Stuart-Smith ethical principles.

We also found that 57 per cent of organisations were training their managers in the art of performance management, and one-third were offering some form of training to all employees. However, we must not be seduced into thinking that the problems addressed by these writers have disappeared. Research linking people management practice to organisational performance found that there is still a significant proportion of organisations not making any real efforts to manage performance and in which the notion of appraisal and review is still in its infancy. Nor can we assume that even the best examples of performance management have fully resolved the problems discussed below.

POSSIBLE RESPONSES BY PRACTITIONERS

The key question is: what can practitioners do to address the issues raised by the commentators? Some suggestions are:

Issue 1: Line management commitment and capability

This is probably the most important issue. If it is not dealt with, performance management will fail. Eight approaches to achieving commitment and capability were described in Chapter 1 (pages 18–19), as summarised below:

- Provide leadership from the top.
- Involve line managers in the design and development of performance management processes.
- Use competence in performance management as a key criterion in assessing managers' performance.
- Use 360-degree feedback or upward assessment to assess the performance management abilities of line managers, and take corrective action as required.
- Survey the reactions of employees to performance management regularly, and take action to deal with weaknesses.
- Provide systematic training in the performance management skills managers need to use.
- Provide continuing coaching and guidance to individual managers to supplement formal training.

Issue 2: Performance management is difficult

This has to be recognised when developing performance management and carrying out the actions set out above to improve the capability of line managers. It is an issue that requires continuous attention. It is not enough to expose managers to a one-day training course on how to set objectives and conduct performance reviews. The management of performance and the skills required to do it must be an integral part of the initial and continuing development programmes for managers. Mentoring, coaching and guidance have to be provided for. It is also not enough simply to train managers in the skills of performance management: they must also understand *why* – particularly what it means for them in terms of being more effective in their management role and achieving their own objectives. In this respect many of our case study organisations had linked performance management to desirable management behaviour. In essence this meant that part of performance management for managers was around how well they managed the performance of their teams.

Issue 3: Poorly designed performance management processes

The design of performance management processes should take into account the following requirements:

- The aims and purpose of performance management are defined.
- How these aims will be achieved is described.
- The involvement of line managers and employees in the design of the system is provided for.
- The use of objectives is determined – the form they should take, how they

will be measured, how individual objectives will be aligned to corporate objectives, and how objectives will be agreed.

- The basis upon which performance planning should take place is defined.
- The use of personal development plans is explained and built into the system.
- Provision is made to ensure that managers and their staff see performance management as a natural process of management which takes place on a continuous basis.
- The approaches to be used in performance management review meetings are defined with an emphasis on the need to avoid a top-down approach and ensure that a genuine dialogue takes place.
- The responsibilities of both parties for preparing for the review as well as taking part in it are defined.
- Consideration is given on how to ensure that performance management is perceived by everyone as a necessary and helpful process of management and development.
- The documentation is designed to be simple and easy to use – bureaucracy is kept to a minimum.
- Consideration is given to whether or not there should be a direct link through ratings to performance or contribution-related pay. If it is decided that there should be a link, decisions are necessary on the use of ratings and how this will avoid prejudicing the developmental purpose of performance management.
- If rating is to be used, consideration is given on how fairness and consistency are achieved.
- The case for using 360-degree or upward appraisal is evaluated.
- The skills managers need to use and how they should be developed are defined.
- A plan for gaining the commitment of line managers and employees to performance management is prepared.
- Methods of design including the use of pilot testing are determined.

Issue 4: Unitary and pluralistic frames of reference

It should not be assumed that line managers and employees will take the same view of what is good for them as held by top management. They will want to know what is in it for them. Their viewpoint must be considered in the design of the scheme. How the concerns of employees are to be met must be considered and explained in the involvement, communication and training programmes that are essential to the effective introduction and continuing use of performance management. Recent research for the CIPD by Nicholas Kinnie and Juani Swart[15] indicates that organisations must understand better how individuals develop their sense of identity, and in particular where their primary source of identity derives from. Is it the employing organisation, the work team, their profession, or the customers they serve? This will then influence the factors that motivate them to perform better, and in particular to share their knowledge and expertise willingly in the pursuit of organisational goals and objectives.

Issue 5: Rhetoric and reality

Rhetoric is defined by the *Concise Oxford Dictionary* as 'language designed to persuade or impress (but perhaps insincere or exaggerated)'. The cynical view is that this is exactly what managements do when they talk about performance management. They don't mean what they say. That may be the case in some organisations but our field work in 1997 and 2004 did not suggest it was a feature in the organisations we visited.

However, we have also found that some organisations believe they are delivering effective performance management when in fact they are operating a fairly mechanistic system of review or rating for performance pay. One of the common failings with regard to performance management is in the area of evaluation. Much of the evaluation of performance management systems rests on *ad hoc* measures or informal feedback. Organisations must ensure that they build in meaningful success criteria if they are going to close the rhetoric reality gap between what they claim for their process and what it actually achieves.

The only response to this issue is for practitioners to recognise that introducing and maintaining performance management is probably one of the hardest tasks they will ever have to undertake. They cannot just design some forms, set out the procedures in a brochure, run some one-day training courses and sit back and expect it to happen. They have to work very hard indeed at ensuring that whatever process they are attempting to introduce is based on very careful and thorough analysis of what the organisation really needs and what it is feasible for line managers and staff to do about it. They must also review it regularly on the basis of evaluation and feedback to ensure that it remains aligned to the needs of the business. Finally, they must make sure they take everyone – both managers and employees – with them all the way, and that the systems continue to be perceived as fair and just for all.

Issue 6: System factors are ignored

The message has to be delivered to line managers that when reviewing performance, they must consider not only what the individual has or has not achieved but also the context in which this performance has taken place and the influence of the system of work and other extraneous factors on that performance. This will include the quality of leadership displayed by managers and their interest in the development of their staff.

Issue 7: Appraisal is an inconsistent process

Inconsistency can happen when rating takes place. This will never be eliminated but it can be alleviated in one or more ways:

- *Forced distribution* – managers are required to conform to a pattern of distributing their ratings. But this is an arbitrary and unpopular method with many weaknesses, and only 8 per cent of the respondents to the CIPD survey used it

- *Ranking systems* – staff are ranked in order of merit and the rank order is divided into segments which indicate ratings – for example, the top 10 per cent are rated A

- *Training* – this can take place in the form of 'consistency' workshops for managers who build a level of common understanding about rating levels

- *Calibration* – groups of managers meet to review the pattern of each other's ratings and challenge unusual decisions or distributions. This is time-consuming but it can be effective

- *Monitoring* – ratings are monitored by HR, which challenges any unusual patterns and identifies and questions what appear to be unwarrantable differences between departments' ratings. This is the approach favoured by many organisations, although there is much to be said for supporting it with training and peer reviews

- *Grandparenting* – individual line manager's ratings or assessments are monitored by their line managers and any anomalies or abnormal patterns are questioned.

Issue 8: Performance management is wrongly focused on financial rewards

Over-emphasis on the link between performance appraisal ratings and pay can indeed reduce the developmental impact of performance management. But it is wrong to assume that performance management is synonymous with performance-related pay. They are often associated, but such a link is not inevitable and our research confirmed that more attention to developmental objectives was given in most of the organisations we visited. Fewer than half (42 per cent) of the respondents to the survey agreed with the statement that pay contingent on performance is an essential part of performance management, whereas 70 per cent believed that the focus of performance management is developmental.

However, if some form of contingent pay is used, performance has to be assessed to inform decisions. One solution to this problem is to de-couple the development and pay reviews. Another is to avoid rating altogether in the developmental review. Yet the prevailing view is that once performance management is linked to reward, more problems are always likely to occur and individuals will find it difficult to be totally open and honest in performance discussions. Methods of deciding on contingent pay without rating are examined in Chapter 7.

Issue 9: Performance management is a means of oppressive or coercive control

This criticism has been made by a number of academic commentators. Their almost obsessive focus on the use and misuse of power gives the impression that they believe organisations are not entitled to have a sense of purpose or a sense of direction, are not entitled to believe that to perform well is better than to perform badly, and are not entitled to define what they mean about performing well. Yet that is what organisations have to do, and it does not seem unreasonable that they should develop processes that will help them to do it.

But there are ways of meeting these requirements without dressing up the use of naked power in the rhetoric of performance. A stakeholder approach which recognises that the diversity of interests is appropriate and which is conducted in accordance with ethical principles and the rules of procedural justice (see Chapter 1) is right. Managements should listen and act on the views of other stakeholders, but to deny the right of managers as stakeholders to define *their* expectations and to implement some form of strategy is unrealistic. It is important that performance management should be underpinned by a set of values and a vision that is strengthened through implementation and review, and that stresses how people can expect to be treated and managed. It should also define a common aim or purpose that can help to unite effort and promote the development of shared goals and objectives. Many of the people we talked to linked performance management to organisational values and reflected these in the behaviours they expected of their managers.

Furthermore, the commentators are referring to old-fashioned performance appraisal schemes in which superiors told their subordinates what to do and what they thought of them. This is certainly not a feature of performance management as practised by the organisations we have contacted in both our research projects. Here it is much more likely that the performance review will be a two-way process, individuals taking active responsibility for their own development and careers.

Issue 10: Line managers and employees tend to be disenchanted with performance management

Some sweeping and unsupported statements have been made by commentators to this effect, and undoubtedly it does happen to a certain extent in all organisations and to a large extent in some organisations. But we found no convincing evidence in either of our research projects that it was a universal phenomenon, as the academics seem to believe. To minimise its occurrence the solution is to pay particular attention to involvement, communication and training when introducing performance management, and to continue to provide support, encouragement and guidance when it is in operation. Most of our interviewees reported that line managers were generally positive about performance management.

If good performance management can be defined as a tool to help line managers carry out their management role more effectively, then organisations must act if line managers are reluctant to use it or are negative about its effectiveness. This can mean one of two things. Either performance management needs reviewing or line managers need to better understand the nature and importance of their people management role.

Endnotes

1 Barlow, G. (1989) 'Deficiencies and the perpetuation of power: latent functions in performance appraisal', *Journal of Management Studies*, September, pp.499–517.

2 Bowles, M. L. and Coates, G. (1993) 'Image and substance: the management of performance as rhetoric or reality?', *Personnel Review*, Vol. 22 No. 2, pp.3–21.

3 Carlton, I. and Sloman, M. (1992) 'Performance appraisal in practice', *Human Resource Management Journal*, Vol. 2 No. 3, Spring, pp.80–94.

4 Deming, W. E. (1986) *Out of the Crisis*. Cambridge, Mass., Massachusetts Institute of Technology, Center for Advanced Engineering Studies.

5 Engelmann, C. H. and Roesch, C. H. (1996) *Managing Individual Performance*. Scottsdale, Ariz., American Compensation Association.

6 Furnham, A. (1996) 'Starved of feedback', *The Independent*, 5 December, p.16.

7 Grint, K. (1993) 'What's wrong with performance appraisal? A critique and a suggestion', *Human Resource Management Journal*, Spring, pp.61–77.

8 Hendry, C., Woodward, S. A., Bradley, P. and Perkins, S. J. (2000) 'Performance and rewards: cleaning out the stables', *Human Resource Management Journal*, Vol. 10 No. 3, pp.46–62.

9 McGregor, D. (1957) 'An uneasy look at performance appraisal', *Harvard Business Review*, May–June, pp.89–94.

10 Newton, T. and Findlay, P. (1996) 'Playing God? The performance of appraisal', *Human Resource Management Journal*, Vol. 6 No. 3, pp.42–56.

11 Stiles, P., Gratton, L., Truss, C. (1997) 'Performance management and the psychological contract', *Human Resource Management Journal*, Vol. 2 No. 1, pp.57–66.

12 Townley, B. (1990/1991) 'Appraisal into UK universities', *Human Resource Management Journal*, Vol. 1 No. 2, pp.27–44.

13 Townley, B. (1990) 'A discriminating approach to appraisal', *Personnel Management*, December, pp.34–7.

14 Winstanley, D. and Stuart-Smith, K. (1996) 'Policing performance: the ethics of performance management', *Personnel Review*, Vol. 25 No. 6, pp.66–84.

15 Kinnie, N. and Swart, J. (2004) *Managing the Careers of Professional Knowledge Workers*. London, CIPD.

4

Performance management in action: outcomes of the CIPD survey 2004

SUMMARY OF FINDINGS

The CIPD survey of performance management in December 2003 covered 506 respondents. The key data emerging from the survey were:

- 87 per cent operated a formal performance management process (37 per cent of these were new systems)
- 71 per cent agreed that the focus of performance management is developmental
- 62 per cent used objective-setting
- 31 per cent used competence assessment
- 14 per cent used 360-degree feedback
- 6 per cent used team appraisal
- 62 per cent used personal development plans
- 59 per cent gave an overall rating for performance
- number of rating levels used:
      three: 6 per cent
      four: 28 per cent
      five: 48 per cent
      six and over: 17 per cent
- 8 per cent used forced distribution to guide ratings
- 55 per cent disagreed that pay contingent on performance is an essential part of performance management
- 43 per cent used ratings to inform contingent pay decisions; 53 per cent did not
- 31 per cent had performance-related pay (only 26 per cent of this group thought it was more than partly effective)

- 7 per cent had competence-related pay

- 4 per cent had contribution-related pay

- 3 per cent had a form of team-based pay

- 46 per cent separated performance management reviews from pay reviews; 27 per cent did not

- 75 per cent agreed that performance management motivates individuals; 22 per cent disagreed

- 26 per cent thought that performance management was bureaucratic and time-consuming

- 75 per cent said that line managers own and operate the performance management process

- the extent to which buy-in to performance management was obtained from line managers was:

completely, all actively in favour	16 per cent
most generally accepted that it was useful	62 per cent
most were indifferent but went through the motions	22 per cent
most were hostile	1 per cent

- 61 per cent of line managers believed that performance management was very or mostly effective; 37 per cent believed it was partly effective or ineffective

- 37 per cent of other staff believed that performance management was very or mostly effective; 59 per cent believed it was partly effective or ineffective

- 42 per cent of respondents agreed that performance management should be distanced as far as possible from payment systems; 56 per cent disagreed.

PERFORMANCE MANAGEMENT SURVEY

The aim of the survey was to gather information on what tools and activities practitioners are using under the banner heading of 'performance management', and on the thinking behind the design of performance management processes. The survey was also concerned with obtaining views on the effectiveness of performance management as a whole and of the various processes involved and on the impact performance management makes. The survey questionnaire is reproduced in Appendix C.

Where possible the results have been compared against the previous performance management survey carried out by the Institute of Personnel and Development (IPD) in 1997. Where specific differences were noted, the results have also been reported by sector.

The results are set out in this chapter under the following headings:

- the profile of respondents
- features of performance management
- the process of performance management
- contingent pay
- rating
- performance data
- who sets the performance requirements for individuals?
- maturity and the development of performance management
- consultation on performance management
- training in performance management
- views on performance management generally
- the attitude of line managers
- evaluation of performance management
- the impact of performance management
- criteria used to measure individual performance
- attitudes to performance management
- the future of performance management
- factors demonstrating positive outcomes
- conclusion.

THE PROFILE OF RESPONDENTS

31 per cent of responses came from the public sector, 24 per cent from private sector manufacturing, 40 per cent from private sector services and 3 per cent from the voluntary sector. A further 2 per cent described themselves as being in some other category. 14 per cent of responses were received from organisations that employed more than 5,000 employees, 28 per cent employed between 1,000 and 5,000, 36 per cent had between 250 and 1,000 employees, and 21 per cent had between 100 and 250.

87 per cent of those who returned the questionnaire operated formal processes to monitor management performance. Of those who did not, 65 per cent had plans to do so in the next two years.

The majority of respondents were operating formal processes for all employees, although managers and professionals were more likely to be included in formal processes than manual, blue-collar, technical or clerical workers. 37 per cent of respondents had different processes for different groups of workers.

Where processes differed, respondents were asked to complete the questionnaire on behalf of the largest group of employees to which formal processes applied. In the majority of cases (53 per cent) this meant managers.

FEATURES OF PERFORMANCE MANAGEMENT

Respondents were asked to indicate what activities featured in their performance management arrangements. They were also asked to indicate whether or not they believed this practice to be effective in raising performance. Their responses are listed in Table 2.

Table 2 | *Features of performance management*

	Percentage of organisations using this feature	Percentage of organisations using this feature who believe it to be effective
Individual annual appraisal	65	83
Twice-yearly/biannual appraisal	27	38
Rolling appraisal	10	21
360-degree appraisal	14	20
Peer appraisal	8	12
Self-appraisal	30	53
Team appraisal	6	10
Subordinate feedback	11	17
Continuous assessment	14	20
Competence assessment	31	39
Objective-setting and review	62	82
Performance-related pay	31	39
Competence-related pay	7	11
Contribution-related pay	4	6
Team pay	3	5
Coaching and/or mentoring	36	46
Career management and/or succession planning	37	47
Personal development plans	62	81

Fewer respondents were carrying out individual annual appraisals than in 1997 when the figure was 85 per cent. Objective-setting and review also appeared to be less popular than in 1997 when 83 per cent of respondents used this process.

360-degree appraisal had grown in popularity since 1997, albeit only from 11 to 14 per cent. Team assessment featured for the first time as a tool for performance management.

The use of performance-related pay dropped from 43 per cent in 1997 to 31 per cent in 2004.

THE PROCESS OF PERFORMANCE MANAGEMENT

Respondents were asked to indicate which of a number of statements best described performance management in their organisations. Their answers are summarised in Table 3.

CONTINGENT PAY

Pay contingent on performance was thought to be more of an issue in the private service sector where 42 per cent of respondents agreed that it was an essential element.

46 per cent of respondents tried to separate performance management from contingent pay reviews. This was most likely to happen in the private service sector and least likely to happen in the public sector – the figures were 55 per cent and 37 per cent respectively.

RATING

59 per cent of respondents said they gave an overall rating for performance. This rose to 68 per cent in private sector manufacturing and 65 per cent in the private service sector, and dipped to 46 per cent in the public sector. The majority (72 per cent) used numerical or alphabetical ratings, but 42 per cent used verbal ratings. The highest use of numerical or alphabetical ratings was in the private sector with the public sector more likely to use verbal ratings. The most common number of levels used for rating was five, used by 47 per cent of respondents.

The most common method used to achieve consistency in ratings was management group review, used by 32 per cent of respondents. Forced distribution was used by only 8 per cent, although it was more popular in the private sector manufacturing sector where 12 per cent reported its use. 18 per cent of respondents used a grandparenting system, 16 per cent workshops or seminars, and 10 per cent utilised prior estimates by the management group.

43 per cent of those who used ratings used them to inform contingent pay decisions. This figure rose to 54 per cent in private sector manufacturing and dipped to 29 and 30 per cent in the not-for-profit and public sectors respectively.

Table 3 | *Description of current performance management process*

	Strongly agree	Agree	Disagree	Strongly disagree
Pay contingent on performance is an essential part of performance management	9%	33%	38%	17%
Line managers own and operate the performance management process	15%	60%	21%	2%
Performance management is an integrated part of the employee-line manager relationship	20%	65%	13%	0%
Performance management is integrated with other people management processes	13%	64%	20%	1%
The focus of performance management is developmental	12%	59%	27%	1%
Performance management integrates the goals of individuals with those of the organisation	21%	63%	13%	2%
Performance management is an integral part of the people management strategy	26%	61%	11%	1%
Performance management motivates individuals	7%	68%	22%	0%
Performance management is used to manage organisational culture	6%	48%	39%	4%
Performance management sets stretching and challenging goals	10%	63%	24%	0%
Performance management is bureaucratic and time-consuming	2%	24%	60%	13%
The aims and objectives of performance management are well communicated and fully understood	5%	57%	34%	1%
Performance management helps us express the value of the people contribution in the organisation	10%	61%	24%	1%

Where ratings were not used to inform contingent pay decisions, a variety of methods were used. 5 per cent used annual increments and 5 per cent a national pay system. Others used industry norms, management opinion and the budget available.

The link between individual and organisational objectives

79 per cent of respondents linked individual and organisation objectives. The methods for linking objectives are listed in Table 4.

Table 4 | *The link between individual and organisational objectives*

	Percentage of organisations using this method to link objectives
Cascade from central business strategy	44
Linked to business plan	12
Appraisal	5
KPI support business objectives	4
Individual goals	4
Team plans	4
Balanced scorecard	3
Financial results	2
Bonus process	2
Other	13
Not stated	11

PERFORMANCE DATA

Performance management data is most likely to be kept by the personnel department (74 per cent of cases). However, 72 per cent of respondents said that line managers kept documentation and 67 per cent said that the individual kept a copy.

WHO SETS THE PERFORMANCE REQUIREMENTS FOR INDIVIDUALS?

In the main senior managers or team leaders are responsible for specifying the performance requirements from individuals. However, there were some notable differences between sectors in that individuals, line managers and personnel were much more likely to take responsibility in the service sector. The full breakdown by sector is given in Figure 5.

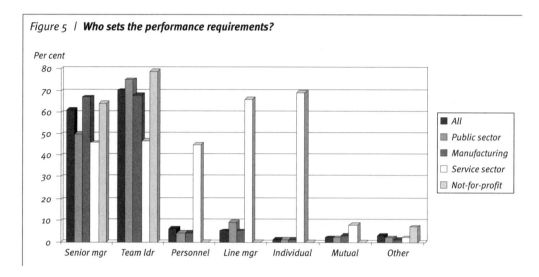

Figure 5 | **Who sets the performance requirements?**

MATURITY AND THE DEVELOPMENT OF PERFORMANCE MANAGEMENT

The majority of respondents were operating a mature system that had been developed over the years, as shown in Figure 6.

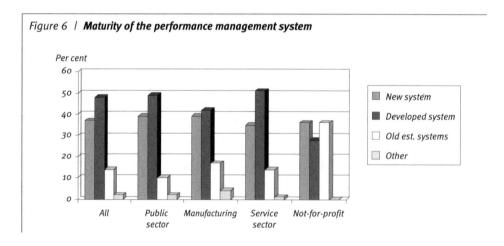

Figure 6 | **Maturity of the performance management system**

46 per cent of respondents said their system took less than one year to develop; 35 per cent took more than one year but less than two; and 14 per cent took more than two years to develop their system. The service and not-for-profit sectors generally took less time to develop their systems.

57 per cent of respondents took less than one year to implement their system; 29 per cent took more than one year but less than two; and 10 per cent took more than two years. The public sector generally took more time to implement their systems, only 40 per cent taking less than one year.

CONSULTATION ON PERFORMANCE MANAGEMENT

Only 23 per cent of respondents consulted all staff on performance management, but 73 per cent consulted senior managers and 57 per cent consulted personnel staff. There were some sector differences (for full breakdown, see Figure 7), with the not-for-profit sector far more likely to consult all staff.

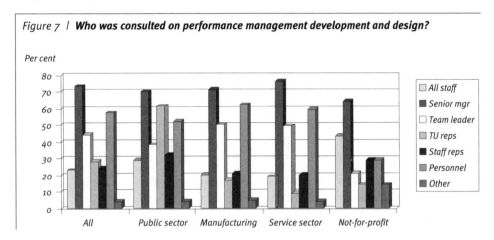

*Figure 7 | **Who was consulted on performance management development and design?***

The most common form of consultation was by briefing session for groups of employees, used by 51 per cent of respondents. 24 per cent have workforce representatives on advisory panels and 45 per cent channelled information and comments through line managers. Only 2 per cent of respondents undertook no consultation at all.

TRAINING IN PERFORMANCE MANAGEMENT

Managers are most likely to receive training in performance management, although only 57 per cent of respondents reported that they conduct such training. 34 per cent trained all staff. The public and not-for-profit sectors are more likely to provide training for all staff (49 and 42 per cent respectively). Only 25 per cent of respondents in the private sector trained all their staff.

VIEWS ON PERFORMANCE MANAGEMENT GENERALLY

The questionnaire began by asking the extent to which respondents agreed or disagreed with a set of statements describing what performance management should be about.

The majority of respondents either agreed or strongly agreed with the following statements about performance management:

- The most important aspect of performance management is the setting of challenging and stretching goals (67 per cent)
- Performance management will only succeed if it is part of an integrated approach to management (98 per cent)

- Performance management will only succeed if it integrates the goals of individuals with those of the organisation (95 per cent)

- It is essential that line managers own the performance management system (93 per cent)

- The focus of performance management is developmental (71 per cent)

- Performance management should be a continuous and integrated part of the line manager/employee relationship (99 per cent)

- Performance management should be about motivating individuals (96 per cent)

- Performance management is an essential tool in the management of organisational culture (94 per cent)

- Everyone must be trained in performance management techniques for any performance management system to be successful (77 per cent)

- It is essential that performance management is accompanied by extensive communication to ensure that its aims are fully understood (94 per cent)

- Quantifiable measures of performance are essential to successful performance management (84 per cent).

There was therefore a great deal of consensus among respondents about the need for performance management to be integrated, owned by line managers and fully understood by everyone involved. This broadly reflected the previous survey carried out in 1997, although the level of agreement is now much higher, particularly on issues of integration and ownership.

THE ATTITUDE OF LINE MANAGERS

62 per cent of respondents reported that line managers generally find performance management useful. However, 22 per cent thought they 'went through the motions', and 1 per cent reported active hostility. 16 per cent said that most were very positive about performancé management.

EVALUATION OF PERFORMANCE MANAGEMENT

50 per cent of respondents said they formally evaluate performance management. The most common process for evaluation was opinion or attitude surveys, used by 56 per cent. Oral feedback from managers was used by 47 per cent, formal written feedback by 39 per cent, and focus groups by 29 per cent.

The key factors used to determine the effectiveness of performance management are shown in Table 5.

Table 5 | Key factors for effectiveness of performance management

	Percentage of respondents giving a 1 or 2 importance rating
Achievement of objectives	50
Achievement of financial targets	25
Development of competence	21
Productivity	19
Development of skills	17
Improved customer care	15
Changes in behaviour	14
Improved quality	13
Motivation	9
Feedback on clarity of purpose	8
Analysis of problems	8
Changes in attitude	6

THE IMPACT OF PERFORMANCE MANAGEMENT

Survey respondents were asked how effective they believed performance management process have proved to be in improving overall performance. Their answers are summarised by sector in Figure 8.

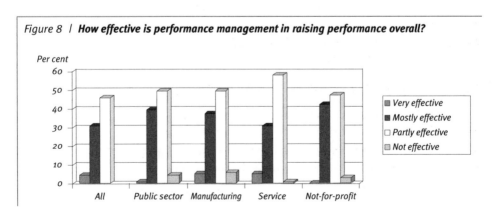

Figure 8 | How effective is performance management in raising performance overall?

CRITERIA USED TO MEASURE INDIVIDUAL PERFORMANCE

Respondents were asked what criteria were deemed most important in their organisation for measuring individual performance. Their answers are set out in Table 6.

Table 6 | Criteria used for assessing individual performance

	Very important	Important	Not very important	Not used as a measure
Customer care	45%	40%	7%	5%
Quality	47%	44%	3%	4%
Flexibility	22%	56%	13%	4%
Competence	53%	40%	3%	2%
Skills/learning targets	18%	57%	16%	4%
Business awareness	17%	52%	21%	6%
Working relationships	35%	53%	7%	3%
Contribution to team	34%	57%	4%	2%
Financial awareness	11%	47%	28%	10%
Productivity	34%	49%	9%	6%
Aligning personal objectives with organisational goals	29%	48%	16%	4%
Achievement of objectives	52%	42%	3%	1%

There was little noticeable difference between the sectors. However, working relationships, customer care and business awareness were considered to be somewhat more important in the service sector.

ATTITUDES TO PERFORMANCE MANAGEMENT

Respondents were asked to rate how various groups within their organisations regarded performance management, and how effective they believed the current process for managing performance to be. The responses are summarised in Table 7.

Table 7 | Attitudes to performance management

	Very effective	Mostly effective	Partly effective	Not effective
Senior managers	14%	60%	22%	3%
Other managers/team leaders	3%	58%	35%	2%
Other staff	1%	36%	51%	8%
Personnel	10%	49%	33%	6%

There was no noticeable difference in attitudes between sectors. In all cases managers seem to be the group generally most positive about performance management.

THE FUTURE OF PERFORMANCE MANAGEMENT

48 per cent of respondents were proposing to make changes to their performance management arrangement within 12 months. Respondents in all sectors were just as likely to be considering change.

Key issues

Respondents were asked to list the three key issues they believed to be important in the introduction, maintenance or improvement of performance management. This question was framed as an open question with no prompts for respondents. Despite this there was a surprising level of agreement about the most important issues. These are summarised in Table 8.

Table 8 | Key issues in performance management

	All	Public sector	Manufacturing sector	Service sector	Not-for-profit sector
Management buy-in	35%	29%	42%	39%	50%
Communication of objectives	35%	34%	35%	34%	21%
Regular evaluation	17%	18%	11%	18%	29%
Training	15%	16%	13%	13%	36%
Simple process	15%	14%	18%	15%	14%
Alignment with business objectives	12%	14%	9%	13%	14%
Follow-up/feedback	11%	8%	14%	12%	0%
Trained line managers/ appraisers	10%	9%	12%	9%	7%
Consistency of use/fairness	10%	11%	12%	9%	7%
Staff understand value	9%	4%	9%	12%	0%
Links to personal development	8%	11%	8%	8%	7%
Joint ownership	6%	7%	4%	8%	0%
Achievable goals	6%	3%	5%	7%	14%

FACTORS DEMONSTRATING POSITIVE OUTCOMES

Finally, respondents were asked what factors they would use to demonstrate positive outcomes from performance management. In previous surveys this has always been the area that had been most difficult for respondents, so once again this was posed as an open question. Respondents demonstrated a diversity of opinion on what successful performance management looks like. Their opinions are summarised in Table 9, which lists all those factors cited by more than 5 per cent of respondents.

Table 9 | Factors demonstrating successful performance management

	All	*Public sector*	*Manufacturing sector*	*Service sector*	*Not-for-profit sector*
Proper discussion/ communication	15%	16%	20%	11%	14%
Increased profitability/ productivity	14%	10%	14%	17%	21%
Achievement of goals	14%	17%	12%	12%	7%
Increased motivation	14%	8%	17%	17%	14%
Regular feedback	14%	11%	16%	13%	28%
Support of personal development	13%	15%	16%	11%	7%
Management buy-in	12%	11%	11%	14%	21%
Alignment with business objectives	12%	16%	16%	9%	7%
Low turnover	11%	7%	12%	10%	14%
Development of skills	10%	8%	12%	10%	14%
Joint ownership	6%	5%	9%	4%	14%
Consistency of approach	6%	5%	7%	6%	0%
Contented workforce	5%	8%	1%	6%	7%
Recognition of over-/under-achievers	5%	4%	5%	6%	7%

CONCLUSION

Overall, there had not been a great deal of movement in the kind of practices employed by organisations to manage performance since the 1997 survey was carried out. Practices such as team appraisal and 360-degree appraisals had become more popular, and it appeared that more organisations had become more sophisticated in their approach and in the integration of performance management with other HR practices. However, the vast majority still relied heavily on the tried and tested practices of objective-setting and review, accompanied by development plans and performance.

5

Performance management and human capital

The concept of human capital has risen to the top of the management agenda in recent years. It is now commonly recognised that plant machinery and other forms of capital only account for a fraction of the true worth of organisations. The remainder is bound up in what is known as 'intangible assets', a large part of which means people or intellectual capital. People and their collective skills, abilities, knowledge and experience, coupled with their willingness to deploy these in the interests of their employing organisation, are now recognised as making a significant contribution to organisational success and as constituting a significant source of competitive advantage. Unlike other forms of capital, human input is very difficult to replicate and is dependent on a complex variety of management, motivation and environmental factors.

To date, although a number of models have been put forward for the evaluation of human capital, actual measures to assess and communicate this value are scarce, and when they do exist tend to measure performance retrospectively using historical data rather than looking forward to likely future performance. Research carried out for the CIPD in 2002 by Professor Harry Scarborough and Juanita Elias[1] found very little commonality between organisations in terms of evaluating their human capital. However, they did find that a number of companies were articulating human capital value by means of some form of competence assessment linked to their wider business environment. They also concluded that there was never likely to be one single measure to determine the contribution of human capital, and that any forms of measurement would have to include a mix of quantitative and qualitative data.

The arguments for meaningful evaluation of human capital are strong. The research carried out for the CIPD by Professor John Purcell and his team at Bath University[2] demonstrated that internal measures of performance are crucial to identifying problems, monitoring progress and linking all aspects of the business through feedback on performance improvement. At the policy level too it has been recognised that meaningful measures of human capital are necessary for informed decision-making on long-term future potential organisational performance. The report from the Accounting for People Task Force set up by the DTI in 2002 and chaired by Denise Kingsmill[3] found widespread agreement for the need for better human capital management reporting and recommended:

> *that directors of companies producing OFRs [Operating Financial Reviews], and all public and other bodies that produce OFRs or reports with similar aims, should include within them information on HCM within the organisation, or explain why it is not material.*

They based this recommendation on the belief that:

> *For most organisations the link between HCM policies and practices and performance is sufficiently central to be a material factor whose disclosure might reasonably be expected to influence assessments of their value and effective stewardship by management. In such cases disclosure increases the value of financial reports and will be important for the effective operation of capital markets.*

The ensuing consultation process on the Operating and Financial Review has taken account of the Kingsmill recommendations. However, it now argues that rather than requiring organisations to report on data that is material to performance, organisations should report information which in their managers' opinion is appropriate. Obviously, there is a difference between 'material' and 'appropriate', but whatever the outcome from the OFR consultation process it would be difficult to argue that performance management data is not an important source of information on human capital and its contribution to business. Ed Lawler[4] has made the point that:

> *It is very difficult to effectively manage human capital without a system that measures performance and performance capability . . . An effective performance management system should be a key building-block of every organisation's human capital management system.*

At the very basic level the performance management process informs organisations how well individuals are achieving their objectives. 62 per cent of the respondents to our survey were using objective-setting as part of the performance management process, and for the majority this meant objectives linked to the business strategy. As part of our case study research we also found that many performance management systems are designed to assess both input to the performance process in terms of the skills and experience that people bring to the job as well as outputs in the form of the achievement of objectives. We further noted that more and more organisations are managing performance not just in terms of what people do but also how they do it. We therefore found behaviour frameworks to be increasingly common, and a number of systems had processes in place to both define and communicate appropriate levels of behaviour to individuals.

At a more sophisticated level, therefore, performance management data can inform on the levels of capability, readiness for promotion or job expansion, the match between required and actual behaviour and competence levels. However, despite this argument that performance management data provides a rich source of material to inform on human capital contribution, we found very little evidence that organisations were making this link. This is the issue we intend to explore in the remainder of this chapter.

INTELLECTUAL CAPITAL

Intellectual capital is commonly held to be the largest contributor in intangible value and is made up of three elements:

- *social capital* – the networks and structures that determine the stocks and flows of knowledge both in and out of the organisation. This may involve the use of communication, involvement and other initiatives to manage knowledge and sometimes also refers to the structure within which human capital is deployed most effectively to apply their knowledge and skills to organisational objectives

- *organisational capital*, defined by Youndt (2000)[5] as the institutionalised knowledge possessed by organisations that is stored in databases, manuals, etc. He argues that this term refers to knowledge that the organisation actually owns. Organisational capital is most likely to be the object of knowledge management systems as organisations strive to find ways to better capture, store, share and use knowledge effectively. It may also cover patents or copyrights that have successfully begun as individual ideas and turned into products

- *human capital*, defined in many different ways by the numerous writers in the field. However, most agree that the term refers to the knowledge, skills and abilities held by the people employed by the organisation, and can be 'made' by developing existing employees or 'bought ' by attracting new staff with the required skills and abilities.

Further analysis of the Bath research data gathered for the CIPD examines how organisations must balance these different forms of capital if they are to manage workers – particularly knowledge workers – for optimum performance. 'Knowledge workers' are defined as workers whose skills or knowledge are inextricably linked with the product or service of their employing organisations. The term therefore embraces such diverse groups as lawyers, accountants, software designers, web designers, academics, marketers and media workers. Increasingly, work is defined by some kind of knowledge element. The management of knowledge workers, according to Juani Swart and Nicholas Kinnie[6] who have carried out this further analysis, rests on the organisation's ability to resolve a number of dilemmas:

- between the retention of knowledge and knowledge workers and the desire of knowledge workers to increase their employability

- between the need to develop organisationally specific knowledge and the wish of knowledge workers to develop transferable knowledge

- between the need for the firm to appropriate the value of that knowledge and the desire by workers to retain their ownership of that knowledge.

They also argue that an understanding of these dilemmas is improved by a greater understanding of where professional workers find their primary source of identity – from their profession, the organisation that employs them, the team or the client. This was an issue that was recognised by some of the knowledge organisations we visited who were employing professional research staff or academics committed to achieving professional status and recognition above any forms of performance recognition that the employing organisation might be able to offer. As Neil Walford, Training and Organisational Development Manager at the Institute of Cancer Research, commented:

> *A lot of people are very self-driven; they want to find an answer. So I guess it's loyalty to the mission, rather than the organisation . . .*

What differentiates human capital from other forms of capital is its precariousness. Unlike other forms of capital it can simply walk away! To realise its potential value we must encourage people to share their talents freely with the organisations that employ them. It is dependent on context, and the skills and experience that may add value in one situation may be worthless in another. All of this makes it difficult to measure and evaluate the contribution of human capital and the return on investments in it such as training and development. There is no universal formula that can be applied in all situations to generate a magical sum to be added to the balance sheet. However, as argued above, performance management generates a huge amount of relevant data. The challenge is how this data can be analysed and assessed together with data from other sources to give a realistic view of human capital contribution.

MODELS OF HUMAN CAPITAL

There is no single framework or recommended best model for the evaluation and measurement of human capital. However, there are a number of models that can give a framework of reference to develop a better understanding of the contribution of human capital. Many of these also recognise that there are many different types of data, both qualitative and quantitative, that must be assessed and analysed to give an accurate understanding of human capital.

The balanced scorecard

As described in Chapter 8, this is one of the best-known methods that attempts to value the people dimension through a number of elements. It is also perhaps the most well-used model for the measurement of the people contribution. Many of the companies studied for both this book and other CIPD research were using some form of the balanced scorecard, often tailored for their own use, for measurement purposes.

One of the major achievements of the balanced scorecard is that it has reinforced the need for better measures of human capital contribution and recognised the contribution of various stakeholders and elements in business success. It also links human capital to other business measures.

Consultancy models of human capital

A number of large consultancy bodies have come up with their own methodologies and models of assessing human capital. Much of the development for these models is based on their consultancy work and is therefore based on a wide range of organisational experience.

Mercer's Human Capital Wheel

The HR consulting company Mercer HR Consulting launched the Human Capital Wheel (see Figure 9) in the 1990s. It was based on a model of organisational performance that explicitly linked human capital management to workforce productivity.

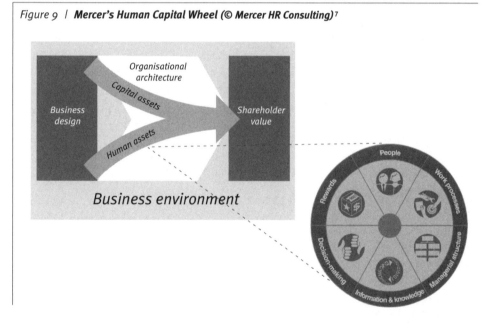

Figure 9 | **Mercer's Human Capital Wheel (© Mercer HR Consulting)**[7]

According to the Mercer model a firm's human capital strategy consists of six interconnected factors:

- people – identifying who is in the organisation, their skills and competencies on hiring, what skills and competence they develop through training and experience, the level of qualifications and the extent to which they apply firm-specific or generalised human capital

- work process – detailing how work gets done, the degree of teamwork, interdependence among organisational units and the role of technology

- managerial structure – reflecting the degree of employee discretion, management direction and control, spans of control, performance management and work procedures

- information and knowledge – how information is shared and exchanged among employees through formal or informal means

- decision-making – how important decisions are made and who makes them; the degree of decentralisation, participation and timeliness of decisions

- rewards – how monetary and non-monetary incentives are used; how much variable pay is at risk; individual versus group rewards, immediate versus career rewards.

Watson Wyatt's Human Capital Index

Watson Wyatt's Human Capital Index proposes that there are four critical HR practices which are linked to increased shareholder value. They are:

- clear rewards and accountability that differentiates between high and poor performers

- a collegial and flexible workplace environment encouraging teamwork and co-operation

- a commitment to hiring the best people and the development of recruitment practices to support the firm's strategic aims

- a level of integrity in communication strategy where goals are clearly stated and business processes have a high level of transparency.

MEASURES OF HUMAN CAPITAL

There are a whole set of measures developed by various different writers which attempt to systematically quantify the human capital of individuals and/or the organisation. These can be summarised as financial approaches that view human capital as having a value which can be added to the bottom line and converted into organisational value, and non-financial approaches that are based on comparisons of various measures of competence.

Many of the approaches to human capital which try to put a value on human assets have arisen from accountancy models. One measure popular in the financial community is 'economic value added' (EVA). Developed by the New York consultancy Stern Stewart & Co., it attempts to link capital budgeting, financial planning, goal-setting, performance measurement, shareholder communication and incentive compensation (Bontis and Dragonetti[8]). The objective is to create a common language of value and a shared understanding of value creation. EVA has been applied to HR by Fitz-Enz,[9] who puts forward the idea that metrics can tell us how future performance can be derived from successful HR systems. These metrics can be summarised as follows:

- how human capital contributes to the value-creating capacity of the organisation
- how process and functions enhance service, quality and productivity
- how human capital is managed – the effectiveness of HR.

Andrew Mayo[10] has done extensive work in this area and argues that people should be viewed as an asset rather than as a cost. He stresses that organisations should create a framework of people-related metrics and strive to quantify both their financial and non-financial value to stakeholders. To enable companies to do this he has developed the 'Human Capital Monitor' for calculating the human asset worth of individual employees. The human asset worth is defined as

$$\frac{employment\ cost \times individual\ asset\ multiplier}{1,000}$$

The individual asset multiplier (IAM) consists of a weighted average assessment of:

- capability
- contribution
- potential
- values alignment.

Mayo then combines this with measures on how successful organisations are at achieving commitment, how good they are at leadership, practical support, the workgroup, learning and development, rewards and recognition, to calculate the people contribution to added value. He stresses that organisations must be careful not to over-engineer the metrics, and favours using relatively few enterprise-wide measures that are specific to creating shareholder value or to achieving current and future organisational goals.

The argument that measures of engagement are important measures of human capital has its origins in research at Sears Roebuck, which investigated the employee customer profit chain. The theory can be summarised as 'Happy workers make happy customers make bigger profits.' This theory is further developed in the people and performance model put forward by Professor John Purcell and his team in the CIPD report *Understanding the People and Performance Link: Unlocking the black box.*[2] This model demonstrated that improvements in employee commitment, job satisfaction and motivation and the drivers of business performance derive from positive HR practices and proactive delivery by well-managed and motivated line managers.

The CIPD Human Capital External Reporting Framework

The CIPD reporting framework,[11] which was based on the research by Professor Harry Scarborough and Juanita Elias in the research report *Evaluating Human Capital*,[1] suggests a number of primary and secondary indicators of the value of human capital. The components of the framework are:

- *human capital strategy* – Reporting should begin with an account of human capital strategy highlighting the overall approach and outlining the vision for the contribution of human capital to future opportunities.

- *acquisition, retention, learning and development, and management* – There should be supporting evidence that should be a balance of both quantitative and qualitative data.

- *information on performance* – There should be data on the effectiveness and performance of human capital and their contribution to the achievement of strategic objectives.

The Council for Excellence in Management and Leadership (CEML) Report[12]

This report was prepared for CEML by the Centre for Business Performance at Cranfield School of Management in 2002. The report argues that:

> it is impractical to expect that a generic set of reporting standards applicable to all organisations can be developed for this area.

The report went on to acknowledge the value of external reporting:

> What investors and other external stakeholders want is insight into the management and leadership talent pool that exists within organisations ...

What the report went on therefore to propose was a range of measures from which organisations can select the key measures that are appropriate to their needs and situations:

A: morale

- absenteeism – across all levels
- accidents – across all levels
- employee turnover
- director and management turnover
- employee satisfaction (staff survey measure)
- sickness – across all levels

B: motivation

- appraisal –completion rates

- percentage of jobholders for whom documented annual appraisal has been agreed
- percentage of jobs for which objectives have been documented
- percentage of jobs for which job descriptions exist
- employee understanding of strategy (staff survey measure)
- employee understanding of vision (staff survey measure)
- employee retention
- director and manager retention
- working hours

C: investment

- benchmarked remuneration levels (external benchmarks)
- director and manager salaries as a percentage of total salaries bill
- human resource spend per employee
- training investment

D: long-term development

- current management and leadership capability
- potential management and leadership capability
- management and leadership skills gaps
- percentage of jobs within level for which emergency cover identified
- percentage of jobs within level for which long-term cover identified
- percentage of jobholders for whom a development plan agreed
- percentage of jobs for which competencies audited
- training days

E: external perception

- job applications: vacancies
- job offers: acceptances

PERFORMANCE MANAGEMENT AS A SOURCE OF HUMAN CAPITAL DATA

The performance management process inevitably generates data that may give insights to the value of human capital, whether or not it is used within the context of one of the models or approaches to measurement summarised above. More than one-third of the respondents to our survey were assessing competence and/or feeding performance data into succession plans and career management. However, when we probed this issue in the case study interviews, only a few had formal and recognised systems in place to capture data that would have had relevance as a measure of human capital. Indeed, the majority view was that performance management information was something that was held between the employee and the line managers and not circulated for wider use.

One organisation that was well advanced in terms of human capital reporting was Norwich Union Insurance. Marie Sigsworth, Director of HR Customer Service, told us:

> We report against 101 different key performance indicators (KPIs) and, obviously, the thing that we are focusing on at the moment is how do you make sure that they are the right ones. Our focus now is on developing indicators that are predictors of performance and drive clear actions rather than retrospective.
>
> We have a 'dashboard', which is the tool the team manager has for assisting planning and allocating work and capturing and graphically reporting on the KPI data. This is used to inform the daily team 'huddles' which focus on performance targets, relevant communications and staff issues. So the team manager can sit with his team and say look our performance stats are right down, what are we doing as a team? How are we going to pull that round? It gives the manager real-time data to work with their team in their huddles, they see it and talk about what they can do.
>
> There's also a productivity measure which the team can talk about in their huddle or can be picked up by the team manager at individual level in one-to-ones or coaching sessions.

'Huddles' in Norwich Union Insurance refer to informal and impromptu team meetings, which are actively encouraged.

Other organisations too have processes for feeding back key performance data into the management decision-making process to inform management activity and behaviour.

THE PRACTICAL APPLICATION OF PERFORMANCE MANAGEMENT TO HUMAN CAPITAL EVALUATION

Given the growing recognition of human capital as a source of organisational value, and the pressure therefore on organisations to collect, analyse and report on their human capital, performance management data is likely to become a key source of information both on the value of human capital and on the management activity needed to manage and deploy this most precious asset.

Performance management data can be used to:

- demonstrate an organisation's ability to raise competence levels
- assess how long it takes for a new employee to reach optimum performance

- provide feedback on development programmes, including induction, coaching and mentoring, in terms of increased performance or capacity to take on new roles
- demonstrate the success of internal recruitment programmes
- indicate how successful an organisation is at achieving its objectives at the individual, team, and department level
- track skills levels and movement in any skills gap in the organisation
- match actual behaviour against desired behaviour
- assess commitment to values and mission
- assess understanding of strategy and contribution.

Most of this information is already captured during the performance management process. To turn it into measure of human capital evaluation, the data has to be processed in a more systematic and widely accessible way. Some practical examples were available from our case study organisations. The use of 'dashboards' as at Norwich Union Insurance, making measures of the people contribution and information available to all managers on a daily basis, was becoming more widespread. This has implications for how performance management is carried out and the requirements for managers to feed good-quality data into effective data management systems.

Endnotes

1 Scarborough, H. and Elias, J. (2001) *Evaluating Human Capital*. London, CIPD.
2 Purcell, J., Kinnie, K., Hutchinson S., Rayton, B. and Swart, J. (2003) *Understanding the People and Performance Link: Unlocking the black box*. London, CIPD.
3 *Accounting for People* (2003), Report from the Task Force to the Secretary of State for Trade and Industry.
4 Lawler, E. E. (2003) 'Current performance management practices', *WorldatWork Journal*, 12 (2), pp.21–30.
5 Youndt, M. A. (2000) 'Human resource considerations and value creation: the mediating role of intellectual capital', Paper delivered at the National Conference of the US Academy of Management, Toronto, August.
6 Swart, J. and Kinnie, N. (2004) *Managing the Careers of Professional Knowledge Workers*. London, CIPD.
7 Nalbantian, Haig. R., Guzzo, Richard A., Kieffer, Dave and Doherty, Jay (2004) *Play to Your Strengths*. New York, McGraw-Hill.
8 Bontis, N. and Dragonetti, N. C. (1999) 'The knowledge toolbox: a review of the tools available to measure and manage intangible resources', *European Management Journal*, 17, pp.391–402.
9 Fitz-Enz, J. (2000) *The ROI of Human Capital: Measuring the economic value of employee performance*. New York, Amacom.

10 Mayo, A. (2001) *The Human Value of the Enterprise: Valuing people as assets – monitoring, measuring, managing.* London, Nicholas Brealey.

11 *Human Capital External Reporting Framework* (2003), London, CIPD.

12 Neely, A., Gray, D., Kennedy, M. and Marr, B. (2002) *Measuring Corporate Management and Leadership Capability.* London, Council for Excellence in Management and Leadership.

6

Performance management and development

PERFORMANCE MANAGEMENT AND LEARNING

To a very large extent people at work learn for themselves from experience (self-managed learning). But they can and should be encouraged and helped to make the best use of that experience. And they will learn more if the environment in which they work is conducive to learning. People also learn from other people. They learn by interaction with their managers and co-workers.

Performance management can play a key role in helping people to learn from their experience, creating a learning environment and ensuring that they receive guidance and support from their managers. The interactions between managers and their staff which take place throughout the year as well as during formal reviews provide opportunities for learning, whether this is an immediate response to a learning situation or the agreement of a longer-term learning or personal development plan.

LEARNING OPPORTUNITIES

Performance management provides specific learning opportunities:

- To be developed so that it becomes more challenging from the viewpoint of new tasks to be accomplished, but also so that the need to acquire or extend knowledge and skills in order to carry out those tasks is revealed.

- Agreement is reached between managers and individuals on 'stretch goals' which can be achieved only if additional learning takes place.

- Specific areas where performance must be improved are identified and the learning required to achieve these improvements is agreed.

- Discussions take place on career opportunities and the learning required to realise them.

- Agreement is reached on how any learning needs that have been established can be met – through self-managed learning, as the individual and the manager work together; through coaching by the manager or by some other source; through the provision of mentoring or through formal training courses inside and/or outside the organisation.

THE ROLE OF LINE MANAGERS

Managers have a key part to play in developing their staff, and performance management helps them to do it. In effect, managers take on a coaching role, although this might be an informal process which progressively serves to increase understanding and develop skills (approaches to coaching were described in Chapter 2).

One of our interviewees explained how in one particular organisation learning is embedded into the performance management process:

We spend a lot of time training and developing managers to manage performance. We put everybody through a coaching programme using the competency frameworks and actively encourage the behaviours we have identified.

One of the competencies in the framework is about developing others, so therefore as a manager they would be assessed on that particular competency.

It's difficult to put in place an objective that you will develop your staff, but because it is assessed and is one of the key competencies for every line manager, it is seen to form an important part of the management role. Obviously, some people are much better at it than others, and for those who aren't it would form part of an individual development plan. For instance, they may need to get better understanding on how to manage performance which is falling below expectations, or they may need to be more effective about the way they identify the training needs or put together the personal development plans.

PERFORMANCE AND DEVELOPMENT REVIEWS AS LEARNING EVENTS

Performance and development reviews, whether conducted formally or informally, can be regarded as learning events. Learning opportunities are provided before, during and after formal meetings.

Prior to reviews

Prior to a review individuals can be encouraged to think about their work experiences and their futures, particularly any career ambitions they might have. They can be asked to marshal their thoughts about what they feel they want to learn, new skills they would like to acquire and the direction in which they want to develop. They can also be asked to think about any specific training from which they believe they could benefit, and whether this will help them in the current job or in progression to the next level. They may be asked to submit their proposals for their own development beforehand or simply to go through a process of reflection enabling them more effectively to discuss their development needs.

During the review

During the review individuals can present to the reviewer their views about what they have learned and what they need to learn. A dialogue between the reviewer and the reviewee can take place in which learning needs can be analysed and a diagnosis agreed in priority areas. Review meetings may also provide an opportunity for coaching. The outcome of the review could be a personal development plan as described below. It is important that any development plans are jointly agreed by the manager and the individual. Individuals must be encouraged to take joint responsibility for their own development and for implementing the outcomes of the learning process.

After the review

Performance management goes on after the formal review. Development plans should be followed by both the individual and the manager. Opportunities may be identified for coaching or further counselling, and both the individual and the manager should take responsibility for putting learning into practice, either by developing the individual's role or by looking for opportunities for him or her to contribute in a different role.

Learning also continues informally. When a manager asks an individual or team to do something, a discussion can take place on how it should be done and what help, in the form of coaching or training, may be required. After the event, an informal analysis can take place of what went well, or not so well, and this can identify further learning needs.

PERFORMANCE MANAGEMENT AND TALENT MANAGEMENT

Talent management is concerned with ensuring that the organisation attracts, retains, motivates and develops the talented people it needs. It is about creating and developing a pool of talented people who are used to operating flexibly and from which successors can be appointed or new roles filled. Performance management can help to identify those with potential and provide the basis for career development and succession planning processes.

Indeed, for many organisations performance management is almost a succession planning tool. We were told the following by our interviewees:

> *It's more about succession than anything else. It's about identifying who are the key people we might want to put into our talent pools and determining where these people might be heading in the organisation.*

and:

> *One of the main things we use appraisal for, rather than just for looking back at the last 12 months and finding out whether targets have been achieved, is career development. We use it to abstract information on training requirements. We also try to use it to help us select people who have potential within the company, either to work overseas or transfer to subsidiaries or for promotion within Head Office functions.*

PERSONAL DEVELOPMENT PLANNING
Defined

Personal development planning is carried out by individuals with guidance, encouragement and help from their managers as required. A personal development plan sets out the actions people propose to take to learn and to develop themselves. They take responsibility for formulating and implementing the plan, but they may receive support from the organisation and their managers in doing so.

Purpose

Personal development planning aims to promote learning and to provide people with the knowledge and portfolio of transferable skills that will help to progress their careers. A distinction can be made between the learning and developmental aspects of personal development plans. Pedler *et al* [1] see learning as being concerned with an increase in knowledge or a higher degree of an existing skill, whereas development is about moving to a different state of being or functioning.

The initial purpose may be to provide what Tamkin *et al*[2] call a 'self-organised learning framework'. But as they comment,

> *within that framework . . . some organisations have interpreted learning widely, encompassing all* aspects *of self-development or included learning activities that have little to do with an individual's current job or even future career. Others have focused heavily on job-related skills or knowledge, or have laid a heavy emphasis on the user's future career and required experience.*

Focus

As the Tamkin *et al* research showed, personal development plans are most commonly focused on job or career development or some mix of both. Less frequently, the emphasis is on the whole person. They comment:

> *Personal development plans which focus solely on skill development for the current job will not be welcomed by many employees. Those which take a broader view of the individual and their future may be more effective for encouraging flexibility and have a higher impact on employees.*

Personal development planning – the overall process

Personal development plans can be created as an outcome of a development or assessment centre. But these may make only a limited impact, and most of the Tamkin *et al* contacts extended the planning process to all their staff or were intending to do so.

Personal development planning has become a well-established feature of performance and development management. It was incorporated in performance management processes by 61 per cent of the organisations responding to the CIPD 2003 performance management questionnaire. 57 per cent of those organisations thought that the planning aspect was very, or mostly, effective, and 23 per cent considered it to be partly effective.

The four stages in preparing a personal development plan are to:

1   identify development needs

2   identify the means of satisfying needs

3   plan action

4   implement.

The approach to personal development planning used by First Direct was described to us by Jane Hanson:

> *It's a framework that details the skills required for different roles based on core competencies. It's an in-house system so it needs constant refreshing, and we need to make sure that that is up to date and reflecting skills required in the business now and in the next five years.*

At the Scottish Parliament a personal development plan (PDP) is an important part of the performance management system. As stated in the description of the scheme,

It is a plan on which to record:

- where the level of competence is met but where we would like to develop further
- any training and/or development needed to support the delivery of that objective.
- any gaps in skills, knowledge or behaviours that need to be overcome in order to meet our objectives.

It gives jobholders and line managers the opportunity to:

- identify, discuss and agree development needs for the year ahead
- prioritise and plan how these will be addressed and achieved
- agree and set dates for reviewing the plan
- if necessary, plan how poor performance might be improved.

Viv Hayward, Performance and Reward Manager, Thames Valley Police HQ, told us that:

> *The strategy driven by the Home Office is that every employee is expected to be fully engaged in the Performance and Development Review (PDR). This is key to the performance management strategy as it establishes strong employment relationships, provides a route to individual, team and organisational performance planning and evaluation, future training and development provision and greater visibility of career paths, competencies and behaviours across roles and ranks. The Integrated Competency Framework, reflected within the PDR, is a tool to enable forces to raise*

standards and quality consistency of performance and behaviour for roles within the Police Service for both officers and police staff.

Identifying development needs

Development needs are identified in performance management processes by individuals on their own or working in conjunction with their managers. This includes reviewing performance against agreed plans and assessing competence requirements and the capacity of people to achieve them. The analysis is therefore based on an understanding of what people do, what they have achieved, what knowledge and skills they have, and what knowledge and skills they need. The analysis is always related to work and the capacity to carry it out effectively.

Individuals can make their own assessment of their personal development needs to get more satisfaction from their work, to advance their careers and to increase their employability.

Identifying the means of satisfying needs

Every organisation we contacted which carries out personal development planning emphasised that it was *not* just about identifying training needs and suitable courses to satisfy them. Training courses may form part of the development plan – but a minor part; other learning activities were much more important.

Examples of development activities include:

- action learning
- coaching others
- distance learning
- e-learning
- formal training courses
- guided reading
- involvement in the community
- involvement in other work areas or secondments
- input to policy formulation
- planned use of a learning resource centre
- seeing what others do (good practice)
- special assignments and project work
- using externally provided learning material
- working with a coach or mentor.

Action planning

The action plan sets out what has to be done and how it will be done under such headings as:

- development needs
- outcomes expected (learning objectives)
- development activities to meet the needs
- responsibility for development – what individuals will do and what support they will require from their manager, the HR department or other people
- timing – when the learning activity is expected to start and be completed
- outcome – what development activities will have taken place and how effective they were
- implementation – how learning will be used and implemented within the organisation and by the individuals.

A personal development plan could be recorded on a simple form under the following headings:

- Career goals, identifying the medium- and long-term work-related aspirations of the individual
- Life goals, reflecting the personal aspiration of the individual
- Job goals, reflecting the aspirations of individuals to grow in their current job in the short or medium term
- Learning and development objectives and outcome expected
- Action to be undertaken, and when
- Support required
- Evidence to demonstrate that activity has been undertaken.

Space should be provided to relate the learning back to the achievement of the individual's goals and aspirations in the short, medium and long term.

The requirement to prepare personal development plans

Most organisations indicate that they expect everyone covered by the planning process to prepare and implement plans. Some, however, take the realistic view that not everyone needs or wants to be involved in elaborate plans, and allow a certain amount of flexibility. In other organisations, personal development planning is encouraged and supported but is not obligatory on the grounds that to insist too strongly on the completion of forms seems to be inconsistent with the principle of self-managed learning. In these organisations, the aim is to help people to understand how they can benefit personally from the process and to emphasise that their managers and the organisation will help them as much as possible to achieve both the work-related and personal goals.

Even where organisations recognise they have a number of staff who are not really interested in career progression, they may take active steps to encourage them to look at what could be available to them. As one HR manager commented:

> *We encourage them to suck it and see. We find that once they discover they are capable of more, they are encouraged to develop themselves further. However, we do not underestimate the contribution of those who just want to remain in the same job and do it well.*

Responsibility for personal development planning

In most applications it is emphasised that individuals are primarily responsible for progressing the plan and for ensuring that they play their part in implementing it. But it is generally recognised that, to different degrees, people will need encouragement, guidance and support. Managers are not expected to sit back and let their staff flounder. They have a role to play in helping as necessary in the preparation and implementation of the plan. They should be expected to:

- help produce action plans which are practical and achievable
- support individuals in their efforts to learn and develop
- offer feedback at appropriate stages
- provide coaching when required
- encourage individuals to expand their horizons and identify the opportunities open to them.

The HR department also has an important part to play, but it is there to provide support rather than direction. The support will include the provision of learning aids, materials and opportunities, the administration of monitoring processes, and advice on methods of learning, on the availability of material and courses (eg e-learning, distance learning) and on the provision of learning support centres.

Implementation

Implementation is mainly the responsibility of the individual – personal development planning is largely about self-managed learning. But managers have a responsibility to provide coaching and support and to organise formal training. They must also ensure that individuals are given the opportunity to implement their personal development plans, which may include time off the job to complete training.

Introducing personal development planning

The introduction of personal development planning should not be undertaken lightly. It is not just a matter of designing a new back page to the performance review form and telling people to fill it in. Neither is it sufficient just to issue guidance notes and expect people to get on with it.

Managers, team leaders and individuals all must learn about personal development planning. They should be involved in deciding how the planning process will work and what their roles will be. The benefits to them should be understood and accepted. It has to be recognised that everyone will need time and support to adjust to a culture in which they have to take more responsibility for their own development. Importantly, all concerned should be given guidance on how people learn, on how to identify learning needs and on the features of the various means of satisfying those needs, and on how they can make use of the facilities and opportunities that can be made available to them.

Endnotes

1 Pedler, M., Boydell, T. and Burgoyne, J. (1989) 'Towards the learning company', *Management Education and Development*, 20(1), pp.1–8.

2 Tamkin, P., Barber, L. and Hirsh, W. (1995) *Personal Development Plans: Case studies of practice*. Brighton, The Institute for Employment Studies.

7

Performance management and reward

[handwritten: PM as component of (reward) package]
[handwritten: Reward as a driver of PM]

PERFORMANCE MANAGEMENT AS A MOTIVATING PROCESS

Performance management, if carried out properly, can motivate people by functioning as a key component of the total reward process. The total reward concept emphasises the importance of considering reward in all its aspects as an integrated and coherent whole. All of the elements of total reward – namely base pay, pay contingent on performance, competence or contribution, employee benefits and non-financial rewards, which include intrinsic rewards from the work itself – are linked together. A total reward approach is holistic, reliance is not placed on one or two reward mechanisms operating in isolation, account is taken of every way in which people can be rewarded and obtain satisfaction through their work. This is done by providing rewards in the form of recognition through feedback, opportunities to achieve, the scope to develop skills, and guidance on career paths. Rewards of this kind can encourage job engagement and promote commitment. All these are non-financial rewards that can make a longer-lasting and more powerful impact than financial rewards such as performance-related pay.

Performance management is, of course, also associated with pay by generating the information required to decide on pay increases or bonuses related to performance, competence or contribution. In some organisations this is its main purpose, but, as we have emphasised several times in this book, performance management is, or should be, much more about developing people and rewarding them in the broadest sense. Approaches to using performance management to motivate by non-financial means are discussed below. The rest of this chapter then deals with performance management and pay. Performance management as a developmental process was considered in more detail in the previous chapter.

PERFORMANCE MANAGEMENT AND NON-FINANCIAL MOTIVATION

Non-financial motivation is provided by performance management through recognition, the provision of opportunities to succeed, skills development and career planning, and by enhancing job engagement and commitment.

Performance management and recognition

Performance management as a continuing process as well as when it is carried out by means of formal or semi-formal reviews is about recognition. Individuals can be informed through feedback about how well they are performing by reference to achievements and behaviours. They can be thanked, formally and informally, for what they have done. They can be helped to understand how they can do even better by taking action to make the best use of the opportunities the feedback has revealed. Recognition takes place during the normal dialogues between managers and their team members, but performance management can also generate information on the use of the more formal approaches that can be used in a recognition scheme, as described later in this chapter.

Performance management and the provision of opportunities to achieve

Performance management processes are founded on joint agreements between managers and their people on what the roles of the latter are and how they can be developed (enriched). It is therefore an essential part of job or role design and development activities.

The planning stage as described in Chapter 2 involves the joint review of the individual's role profile to agree expectations in the form of key result areas, knowledge and skill requirements and behaviours. When agreeing objectives (work or personal) the aim is to stretch people to achieving more. This could be in general terms, but role development should be more about identifying areas in which people can do more to their own satisfaction as well as meeting work requirements (job enrichment). Thus additional projects can be agreed which involve the development of skills and provide the opportunity to achieve and to be recognised for so doing. The role can be enlarged by adding responsibilities – within reason and subject to the agreement of the individual and the guarantee of additional support, coaching and training as required.

Performance management and skills development

Performance management can provide a basis for motivating people by enabling them to develop their skills. Performance development plans as described in the last chapter are a formal means of doing this, but informal interactions between managers and individual provide opportunities for skills development by coaching and guidance. People are said to learn best by doing, but it is more effective if there is an agreed framework for coaching and support to enhance and focus the learning.

Performance management and career planning

Performance management reviews provide opportunities to discuss the direction in which the careers of individuals are going, and what they can do – with the help of the organisation – to ensure that they follow the best career path for themselves and the organisation. This is linked to talent management activities which aim to identify and nurture the present and future talents required by the organisation in the form of skilled and motivated people. It is also often linked to retention strategies as organisations strive to enhance the careers of their most talented people to prevent them from looking for more challenging and stimulating job opportunities elsewhere.

Performance management and job engagement

People experience job engagement when they have interest in and a sense of excitement in the job. This can be created by performance management when it concentrates on intrinsic motivating factors such as taking responsibility for job outcomes, job satisfaction and the achievement and fulfilment of personal goals and objectives. The job can then be enhanced and shaped towards both the needs of the individual and the organisation when the outcomes of this sort of performance management discussion is used as the basis for job or role design, as mentioned above.

Performance management and commitment

One of the prime aims of performance management is to promote commitment to the organisation and its goals by integrating individual and organisational objectives. As we noted from our research, organisations are increasingly using performance management as a means of getting people to uphold the organisation's core values – 'to live the values', as one company told us. We therefore commonly found performance management to be underpinned by a set of core values. As one HR manager put it:

> *Performance management is at the heart of what we do. It is how we shape behaviour and ensure that everyone is aware of what we stand for.*

Non-financial rewards at Centrica

Joe Dugdale, HR Director, Centrica Telecommunications, explained that in Centrica:

> *There are a number of informal reward schemes throughout the organisation. We need to work on the culture: that is where we get the extra performance. If people believe the organisation is managing their career and giving them the opportunity to progress on the back of their potential and high performance, then I think the message is very strong in terms of generating extra contribution. We believe we are trying to build the kind of leadership that motivates and makes people want to put in extra effort, and the kind of culture where people feel valued and feel they have the opportunity to develop. Our values guide behaviour that make people think this is the right place for them.*

THE LINK BETWEEN PERFORMANCE MANAGEMENT AND PAY

As the CIPD survey demonstrated, performance management is not inevitably associated with pay, although that is often assumed to be the case. Only 42 per cent of respondents to the survey had contingent pay. The proportion in public sector organisations was even less – 29 per cent.

The research, however, showed that contingent pay – that is, paying for performance, competence or contribution – is still an important element in many performance management schemes. This is because contingent pay is regarded by many organisations as desirable for three reasons:

- It is fair and equitable to reward people differentially according to their performance, competence or contribution.

- It delivers the message that performance and competence are important.

- It motivates people to perform better or to develop their skills and competencies.

The first reason is undeniable. Most people, including many trade unionists, accept the principle that better people should be paid more. The second reason has some merit, although there are other and possibly better ways of delivering this sort of message – for example, through performance management. The third reason is questionable. It has never been possible to prove that the limited amount of money available in most contingent pay schemes can motivate by providing an incentive. Indeed, research projects such as that conducted by Marsden and French[1] indicated that although a few people who got a meaningful amount of performance pay might be motivated by it, the majority of people who did not were actively demotivated. Performance pay therefore made a negative rather than a positive impact.

This may not always be the case, but the problem with contingent pay is not that the principle is faulty but that the practice is flawed. It is very difficult to manage it well, and what is most likely to go wrong is performance management. This is supposed to generate unbiased and acceptable ratings to determine contingent pay decisions but is often perceived by people to be operated by line managers unfairly, inequitably, inconsistently and with an almost complete lack of transparency. Whether these perceptions are justified or not is immaterial. That is what many people feel, and that is why contingent pay schemes often fail. Organisations tend to rush into contingent pay without appreciating that it all depends on effective performance management processes which are trusted by those whom they affect. It is absolutely essential to get performance management right first, which means ensuring that line managers are capable of handling it properly. And this takes time and effort. To introduce a contingent pay scheme or extensively revise an existing scheme may take three years or more if performance management processes need to be improved and the capability – and willingness – of line managers to operate them properly developed.

A further difficulty with the use of performance management to inform pay decisions is that the most typical approach is performance appraisal, which generates ratings to inform contingent pay decisions, often through a formula (a pay matrix). This may conflict with the developmental purposes of performance management – the performance review meeting will focus on the ratings that emerge from it and how much money will be forthcoming. Issues concerning development and the non-financial reward approaches discussed earlier will be subordinated to this preoccupation with pay. As Nigel Turner, Director of Human Resources at the Royal Free Hampstead NHS Trust, told us:

> *It has always been my view that linking your appraisal system to people's pay distorts the outcome. You lose a lot of the value, both in terms of having a frank discussion and in terms of identifying developmental needs.*

Many organisations attempt to get over this problem by holding development and pay review meetings on separate dates, often several months apart (decoupling). Some try to do without formulaic approaches (ratings and pay matrices) altogether, although it is impossible to dissociate contingent pay completely from some form of assessment.

APPROACHES TO CONTINGENT PAY

That said, many organisations still have contingent pay. Senior managers, politicians, local authority members and charity trustees seem to want it, because, perhaps naively, they believe it provides a direct incentive. The question may be asked: 'What's the alternative?' It is not an easy one to answer. Either pay progression is dependent entirely on service – 'being there' – or spot rates are used with no provision for progression. Neither of these is attractive. So the best has to be made of a bad job – and this means considering what approaches to contingent pay are available that are likely to fit best in the organisation, and what the implications are for performance management.

The CIPD 2003 Reward Management Survey[2] found that 23 per cent of respondents had performance-related pay, only 6 per cent had competence-related pay, and 63 per cent had contribution-related pay. These approaches are summarised below.

Performance-related pay

Performance-related pay provides individuals with financial rewards in the form of increases to basic pay or cash bonuses that are linked to an assessment of performance, usually in relation to agreed objectives. Scope is provided for consolidated pay progression within pay brackets attached to grades or levels in a narrow-graded or career family structure or zones in a broad-banded structure. Such increases are permanent – they are seldom if ever withdrawn.

Alternatively or additionally, high levels of performance or special achievements may be rewarded by cash bonuses which are not consolidated and have to be re-earned. Individuals may be eligible for such bonuses when they have reached the top of the pay bracket for their grade, or when they are assessed as being fully competent, having completely progressed along their learning curve. The rate of pay for someone who reaches the required level of competence can be aligned to market rates according to the organisation's pay policy.

The rate and limits of progression through the pay brackets are typically but not inevitably determined by performance ratings, which are often made at the time of the performance management review but may be made separately in a special pay review.

Performance-related pay has had a bad press and in its pure output form, as described above, is being replaced in many organisations by contribution-related pay, as the CIPD data show.

Competence-related pay

People receive financial rewards in the shape of increases to their base pay by reference to the level of competence they demonstrate in carrying out their roles. It is a method of paying people for the ability to perform now and in the future which is often linked to competency frameworks.

The notion of competence-related pay was initially greeted with enthusiasm as a more acceptable approach than performance-related pay, which could be an integral part of a competency development programme. But it has not been taken up to any great extent because it appears to ignore performance (outcomes) and because the assessment of competence levels as the sole determinant of pay increases has proved to be difficult. One exception to this is the new NHS system introduced in their pay modernisation project, Agenda for Change. As described by Nigel Turner at the Royal Free Hampstead NHS Trust:

> The NHS knowledge and skills framework is linked to the pay system. In this system, every grade has got two bars ('gateways'), one at the end of the first year and one towards the top of the scale. To cross the bar, individuals have to review their knowledge and skills with their manager – and this means that there is more focus on competencies than is currently the case.

Contribution-related pay

Contribution-related pay combines performance- and competence-related pay by rewarding people for both their performance (outcomes) and their competence (inputs). It focuses on what people in organisations are there to do – that is, contribute by their skill and efforts to the achievement of the purpose of their organisation or team.

Contribution-related pay is a holistic process, taking into account all aspects of a person's performance. The case for it was made by Brown and Armstrong:[3]

> Contribution captures the full scope of what people do, the level of skill and competence they apply and the results they achieve, which all contribute to the organisation's achieving its long-term goals. Contribution pay works by applying the mixed model of performance management: assessing inputs and outputs and coming to a conclusion on the level of pay for people in their roles and their work; [relating] both to the organisation and . . . the market; considering both past performance and their future potential.

The approach of the National Crime Squad to contribution pay was described to us by Dave Hays, HR Manager:

> *Salary progression for police staff across the service, and within the National Crime Squad, has traditionally been managed on a 'time served' basis. To explain, a new starter would enter on the first point of a pay band and, come each April, would move up to the next point until they hit the top of the band. Generally speaking, it didn't matter whether the member of staff was good, bad or indifferent – come April they got a pay rise.*
>
> *We challenged this approach by capitalising on the wording contained within the Police Staff Council Handbook, which actually states that:*
>
> 1 *Progression through a scale will normally be by one pay point each year subject to satisfactory performance*
>
> 2 *Progression may be accelerated within the scale for excellent performance, and*
>
> 3 *Progression through a scale may be delayed in cases of poor performance.*
>
> *The salary progression scheme we developed links progression not to performance but to contribution. The focus, largely, is on what you bring to the job, not what you produce at the other end.*
>
> *For salary progression purposes, members of staff will be given a rating against a series of competency areas from the following options: 'competent', 'developing' or 'not met'. Where a member of staff receives a rating of 'competent' against all of the relevant competency areas and they have achieved their key accountabilities they will proceed to the top of their pay band. We anticipate that the majority of people will take approximately 18 months to progress to target salary. Where pay is the incentive to do well, this approach will provide a short-term fix. We do recognise, however, that people may decide to leave after two or three years because they have reached the top of their pay band. If that is the case, then so be it – we view a degree of turnover as quite healthy. That said, we are constantly exploring ways of opening up avenues that will enable people to remain with the NCS – we are working closely with our Career Development Advisor who has recently developed our Career Development Strategy.*
>
> *We've made it clear to people that they can really help themselves by making effective use of our Personal Development and Performance Review Scheme, which can be used to inform salary progression.*

RECONCILING PERFORMANCE MANAGEMENT AND PAY

The problem of reconciling the developmental aspects of performance management or appraisal and pay has been with us for decades. Armstrong commented as long ago as 1976[4] that:

> *It is undesirable to have a direct link between the performance review and the reward review. The former must aim primarily at improving performance and, possibly,*

> *assessing potential. If this is confused with a salary review, everyone becomes over-concerned about the impact of the assessment on the increment . . . It is better to separate the two.*

Many people since then have accepted this view in principle but have found it difficult to apply in practice. As Kessler and Purcell[5] argue:

> *How distinct these processes [performance review and performance-related pay] can ever be or, in managerial terms, should ever be, is perhaps debatable. It is unrealistic to assume that a manager can separate these two processes easily, and it could be argued that the evaluations in a broad sense should be congruent.*

And Armstrong and Murlis[6] comment that:

> *Some organisations separate entirely performance pay ratings from the performance management review. But there will, of course, inevitably be a read-across from the performance management review to the pay-for-performance review.*

The issue is that if you want to pay for performance or competence, you have to measure performance or competence. And if you want, as you should do, the process of measurement to be fair, equitable, consistent and transparent, then you cannot make pay decisions, on whatever evidence, behind closed doors. You must convey to individuals or teams how the assessment has been made and how it has been converted into a pay increase. This is a matter of procedural justice, the rules of which, as expressed by Leventhal,[7] are:

1   *The consistency rule:* the allocation processes should be consistent across people and across time.

2   *The bias-suppression rule:* personal (concealed) self-interest and blind allegiance to narrow preconceptions should be prevented at all costs in the allocation process.

3   *The accuracy rule:* it is necessary to base the allocation process on as much good information and informed opinion as possible.

4   *The correctability rule:* opportunities must exist to modify and reverse decisions made at various points in the allocation process.

5   *The representativeness rule:* all phases of the allocative process should reflect the basic concerns, values and outlook of important sub-groups in the population of individuals affected by the process.

6   *The ethicality rule:* procedures must be compatible with the fundamental moral and ethical values accepted by oneself. Respectful, neutral and trustworthy treatment from authorities must be seen as fair.

Procedural justice demands that there is a system for assessing performance and competence, that the assessment should be based on 'good information and informed opinion', that the person affected should be able to contribute to the process of obtaining evidence to support the assessment, that the person should know how and why the assessment has been made, and that the person should be able to appeal against the assessment.

It therefore seems almost impossible to avoid some sort of assessment or rating in the performance review meeting. The argument that this will not affect the quality of that meeting in terms of its developmental purposes has been dismissed by some people on the grounds that there should be no problem if the reasons for the rating are fully explained (procedural justice) and rating could *enhance* the developmental aspect of the review meeting if it clearly establishes what people have to do or learn to improve their ratings. This sounds reasonable enough, but the evidence from our research was that rating systems were generally, and in some cases, passionately, disliked because they were likely to be unfair and were impossible to understand (or accept). It seems that managers *should* be good at explaining things but don't always do it very well.

This is a thorny problem. But it was interesting to note from the CIPD research that 52 per cent of the respondents with performance-related pay did not have rating.

Three examples of companies who have operated performance management and pay processes without ratings are BP Exploration, Halifax BOS and Zeneca. One approach is for managers to propose where people should be placed in the pay range for their grade, taking into account their contribution relative to others in similar jobs and the relationship of their current pay to market rates. This should be carried out separately from the performance review, with individuals given the opportunity to discuss their manager's proposal and to advance reasons why they should be paid more, and managers expected to respond and to take account of these submissions.

This approach has much to commend it. Even if organisations do not want to go as far as that, there are strong arguments for a separate assessment process which could simply place people in a number of broad categories such as exceptional, consistently good, improvable, and not acceptable. These categories could inform pay decisions.

An interesting approach is adopted at First Direct, described by Jane Hanson:

> *We have spot rates for a base-pay structure and they are based on market information for the role. In addition, there is variable pay which is performance-related. The information for variable pay is drawn through objectives and appraisals, and individuals are allocated a personal performance factor based on their performance. This goes into a formula with a factor that represents the business performance and a target award that represents their level within the organisation. The outcome is a monetary award. We have a calculator on the intranet system so people can put in their salary and personal performance factor and it produces the estimated bonus for them. It's all open.*

Julie Hill, HR Partner, Retail Sales, Retail Development and HEA Central Sites, HBOS, described their approach to pay:

> *We look at a number of things when making a decision about an individual's pay. One will be the size of the role as determined by job evaluation, and we also consider market data and location to determine the average salary that you would expect to pay for that role. We then look at how the individual has performed over the last 12 months. Have they contributed what was expected of them? Have they contributed above and beyond in comparison to their peers? Have they under-performed against what was required of them? These are not ratings: they are just guidelines given to managers to help them assess whether the individual should be given an average, above-average or below-average increase. We have a devolved budget, and managers have to make decisions regarding what percentage should be given to individuals. We suggest that if, for example, a manager has six people carrying out the same roles, then from an equal pay point of view, if they are delivering at the same level and are all competent, they should be getting similar salaries. Individuals paid below the market rate who are performing effectively may get a bigger pay rise to bring them nearer the market rate for the role.*

LINKING PERFORMANCE MANAGEMENT TO PAY DECISIONS

Paul Williams, Group HR Director, Smith & Nephew, expressed his view on the link between performance management and pay quite forcibly:

> *Pay determination should be right at the end of the performance review process. It should be regarded as an outcome but not as the prime driver. I am also very wary of the use of codings in the performance management process; it is too easy to hide behind performance codes and notions of average distribution to avoid a proper interaction with the appraisee about performance and development needs. I accept that performance codings can have an important role to play for calibration purposes but they must not be allowed to undermine or taint the quality of the review discussion.*

The problem of prejudicing performance management as a developmental process by linking it to performance pay decisions has been dealt with by many organisations – 46 per cent of the respondents to the CIPD 2003 survey[2] – by separating (decoupling) the performance and pay reviews. However, some organisations reject the idea of a separate meeting because it imposes an extra burden on line managers. Others believe that the distinction is false and the fact that there will be an assessment or rating of performance at some time in the future will be obvious and is just as likely to prejudice the review meeting as if it had taken place at the same time. The evidence from the focus groups we conducted as part of our 1997 research project is that ratings for pay purposes do seriously prejudice the developmental aspects of performance management. We have to conclude that the two can never be totally separated because there will always be an inevitable read-across. However, if organisations are to have any meaningful discussions about development needs, they must decouple performance review from pay review as much as possible, and so the case for a gap of several months is a strong one.

RECOGNITION SCHEMES

The total reward concept is based on understanding the needs and expectations of employees in order to motivate them and obtain their total co-operation, on the basis that this leads to financial success for the organisation and personal fulfilment for employees. Appropriate recognition of employees plays a vital role in this. Recognition is about saying 'thank you' for a job well done, and thereby motivating the recipient to continue to do those things that benefit the organisation. Recognition will not necessarily motivate the unmotivated employee, but it can reinforce the motivated, encourage and reassure those who are trying to succeed, and prevent previously committed employees becoming demotivated as they think their efforts are not noticed. Performance management processes should identify where special efforts should be made to recognise achievements either during the course of day-to-day work or during formal reviews.

At the most basic level, recognition is free. It does not cost the organisation or its managers anything except for the two minutes it takes to say 'Well done, and thanks,' in person or by e-mail, or the fifteen minutes it takes to write a brief note of appreciation, yet it speaks volumes. More complex recognition programmes – those organisation-wide schemes that offer a fat cheque or generous prize – can work well if well designed, but they can all too easily miss the boat if by focusing on the few they alienate the many.

Yet effective recognition rests on the efforts of the manager. Some managers apparently effortlessly recognise the contribution of their staff and establish positive working relationships. Others find it more of a challenge: praise that is given falsely or negatively – 'That was great, but ...' – is worthless. The ability to recognise and reward effort is therefore a key part of the manager's role and should be reflected in their development and training,

Informal recognition

In an organisation with a large proportion of comparatively low-paid employees, it is important to have a relatively informal recognition scheme, with a greater number of recipients of fairly frequent moderate- to low-cost awards. It can be argued that it is always better to give 1,000 people £10 than one person £10,000.

Informal recognition schemes are not competitive (and nor should they be). Every person, team or group who meets the standard or who does an excellent job should benefit. Kohn (1993) argues strongly against any system that creates 'winners' because 'for each person who wins, there are many others who have lost'.

Formal recognition

Recognition schemes may involve some form of public recognition, such as through an intranet, house journal, noticeboard or an 'Employee of the Month' scheme. Approaches such as these tell everyone about particular achievements or effective contribution.

Formal recognition schemes can also provide individuals (and importantly, through them, their partners) with tangible means of recognition in the forms of gifts, vouchers, holidays or trips in the UK or abroad, days or weekends at health spas, or meals out. Team awards may be through outings, parties and meals. Such schemes may be centrally driven (with a formal nomination process and regular award ceremonies) or devolved to line managers, providing them with the authority and an associated budget to recognise individuals or teams in accordance with guidelines.

Winners of formal awards report that the benefits last longer than the actual prize, because they are offered the opportunity to meet people and take part in projects they would not have previously been considered for, as well as improving their promotion prospects.

The key with formal schemes is to ensure that the award fits the achievement, the award is made to the right people, and that it is 'felt fair'. Whereas it is highly motivating to be formally recognised for a major achievement (eg for successful completion of a project or finalising a major sale), it may be demoralising and demotivating for someone to feel that recognition has been given elsewhere for something he or she has accomplished.

Endnotes

1   Marsden, D. and French, S. (1998) *What a Performance: Performance-related pay in the public services*. London, Centre for Economic Performance.

2   Chartered Institute of Personnel and Development (2003) *Reward Management 2003: A survey of policy and practice*. London, CIPD.

3   Brown, D. and Armstrong, M. (1999) *Paying for Contribution*. London, Kogan Page.

4   Armstrong, M. (1976) *A Handbook of Personnel Management Practice*. London, Kogan Page.

5   Kessler, I. and Purcell, J. (1992) 'Performance-related pay: objectives and application', *Human Resource Management Journal*, Vol. 2 No. 3, Spring, pp.6–33.

6   Armstrong, M. and Murlis, H. (1998) *Reward Management*, 4th edn. London, Kogan Page.

7   Leventhal, G. S. (1980) 'What should be done with equity theory?', in G. K. Gergen, M. S. Greenberg and R. H. Willis (eds) *Social Exchange: Advances in theory and research*, New York, Plenum.

8

Managing organisational performance

The management of organisational performance is, of course, the continuing responsibility of top management who plan, organise and control activities and provide leadership to achieve strategic objectives and meet the needs of stakeholders. An important part of their responsibilities is to monitor performance so that opportunities can be exploited or corrective action taken to deal with shortfalls. That all depends on the existence and proper use of effective measurements. This chapter is therefore primarily concerned with approaches to the measurement of organisational performance.

There are various types of measures, but whichever approach is adopted it is essential to ensure that managers use them sensibly. At Norwich Union Insurance a 'dashboard' (a display of control information on the intranet) is used to inform the daily team 'huddles'. This is described to us by Marie Sigsworth, Director of HR Customer Service:

> *This helps ensure that the relevant information is available to managers on a daily basis. It's what they use to manage their teams. The managers will get together with their teams and discuss what the data is telling them and any ideas they may have to overcome problems and improve the service to our customers. Both managers and team should come away from the meetings knowing what they need to focus on. The focus for the team manager is to ensure there is nothing blocking the service that the team gives to its customers. We call these meetings daily 'huddles'.*

> *So by providing managers with structured information around the balanced scorecard data we are continuously reporting back to them and giving them a greater understanding and feel for what they need to do to increase the contribution of their people – to develop the human capital.*

TYPES OF MEASURES – ORGANISATIONAL

Jack Welch, former CEO of the General Electric Company, used to say that the three most important things you need to measure in a business are customer satisfaction, employee satisfaction and cash flow. These basic considerations govern the various approaches to performance measurement – namely, the balanced scorecard, the

European Foundation for Quality Management (EFQM) model, the economic value added, and other traditional financial measures which are described below.

The balanced scorecard

The concept of the balanced scorecard as originally developed by Kaplan and Norton[1] addresses this multiple requirement. They take the view that 'what you measure is what you get', and they emphasise that

> *no single measure can provide a clear performance target or focus attention on the critical areas of the business. Managers want a balanced presentation of both financial and operational measures.*

Kaplan and Norton therefore devised what they call the 'balanced scorecard' – a set of measures that gives top managers a fast but comprehensive view of the business. Their scorecard requires managers to answer four basic questions, which means looking at the business from four related perspectives:

- How do customers see us? (customer perspective)

- What must we excel at? (internal perspective)

- Can we continue to improve and create value? (innovation and learning perspective)

- How do we look at shareholders? (financial perspective).

Kaplan and Norton believe that the balanced scorecard approach 'puts strategy and vision, not control, at the centre'. They suggest that although it defines goals, it assumes that people will adopt whatever behaviours and take whatever actions are required to achieve those goals:

> *Senior managers may know what the end result should be, but they cannot tell employees exactly how to achieve that result, if only because the conditions in which employees operate are constantly changing.*

They claim that this approach to performance management is consistent with new initiatives under way in many companies in such areas as cross-functional integration, continuous improvement, and team rather than individual accountability.

Kaplan and Norton emphasise that building a scorecard enables a company to link its financial budgets with its strategic goals. They emphasise that the balanced scorecard can help to align employees' individual performance with the overall strategy:

> *Scorecard users generally engage in three activities: communicating and educating, setting goals, and linking rewards to performance measures.*

They quote the exploration group of a large oil company (Shell) which has developed a technique to enable and encourage individuals to set goals for themselves that are consistent with the organisation's. These 'personal scorecards' contain three levels of information:

- corporate objectives, measures and targets
- business unit targets (translated from corporate targets)
- team/individual objectives and initiatives.

Teams and individuals are expected to define how their objectives are consistent with business unit and corporate objectives, to indicate what initiatives they propose to take to achieve their objectives, to list up to five performance measures for each objective, and to set targets for each measure. This personal scorecard is a method of communicating corporate and unit objectives to the people and teams performing the whole. It 'communicates a holistic model that links individual efforts and accomplishments to business unit objectives' (Kaplan and Norton, 1996b). It can therefore be incorporated as a performance management process at individual, team, unit and corporate levels.

To summarise, Kaplan and Norton (1996a) comment that:

Many people think of measurement as a tool to control behaviour and to evaluate past performance. The measures on a balanced scorecard, however, should be used as the cornerstone of a management system that communicates strategy, aligns individuals and teams to the strategy, establishes long-term strategic targets, aligns initiatives, allocates long- and short-term resources and, finally, provides feedback and learning about the strategy.

The Norwich Union Insurance experience

Marie Sigsworth, Director of HR Customer Service, explained to us how Norwich Union used the balanced scorecard.

It's not the typical model you read about in the textbooks but one we have customised for our own use. Norwich Union Insurance has a balanced scorecard, and each of the business units has one as well. It puts equal focus on morale, service and profit. The morale section is really our people section, and it is where all of our people interventions sit. The ultimate aim of all three sections is to raise performance.

The balanced scorecard looks forward four years with clear aims and objectives. This then cascades down into team and individual objectives. Our Chief Executive is very keen about developing a clear line of sight, ensuring that everyone in the organisation understands how they can make an impact on a particular aim or objective within NUI.

Everything is connected to the balanced scorecard. Under the morale section we have performance management, succession planning, learning and development. Also within the balanced scorecard we have developed a number of measures to assess how we are doing at a number of levels. For example, we have developed a leadership survey which we do on a quarterly basis. We ask each of the team 'What do you think of the way that your team manager leads you?' Overall the balanced scorecard drives a focus on the customer and through increased morale and customer satisfaction puts us in a win/win situation.

The European Foundation for Quality Management (EFQM) model

The EFQM model, as shown in Figure 10, indicates that customer satisfaction, people (employee) satisfaction and impact on society are achieved through leadership. This drives the policy and strategy, people management, resources and processes that lead to excellence in business results.

Figure 10 / *The European Foundation for Quality Management (EFQM) model*

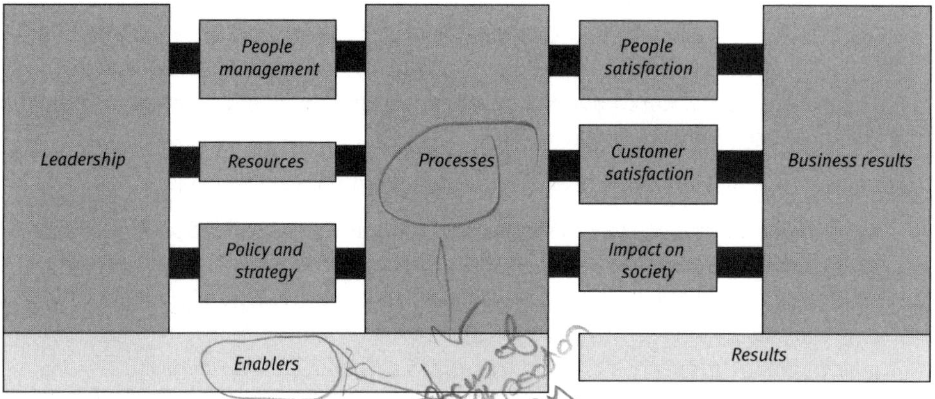

The nine elements in the model are defined as follows:

- *Leadership* – how the behaviour and actions of the executive team and all other leaders inspire, support and promote a culture of total quality management

- *Policy and strategy* – how the organisation formulates, deploys and reviews its policy and strategy and turns it into plans and actions

- *People management* – how the organisation realises the full potential of its people

- *Resources* – how the organisation manages resources effectively and efficiently

- *Processes* – how the organisation identifies, manages, reviews and improves its processes

- *Customer satisfaction* – what the organisation is achieving in relation to the satisfaction of its external customers

- *People satisfaction* – what the organisation is achieving in relation to the satisfaction of its people

- *Impact on society* – what the organisation is achieving in satisfying the needs and the expectations of the local, national and international community at large

- *Business results* – what the organisation is achieving in relation to its planned business objectives and in satisfying the needs and expectations of everyone with a financial interest or stake in the organisation.

Organisations which adopt the EFQM model accept the importance of performance measurement and work all the time to improve the usefulness of their measures, but they also recognise that simply measuring a problem does not improve it. Managers can often devolve their best energies to the analysis, leaving little left for the remedy. The key, they say, is to focus on the *enablers* and the *processes*.

The EFQM model can help performance management by:

- developing a fuller understanding of how business results are achieved and processes continually improved
- offering mechanisms for tackling systems problems in the workplace
- promoting performance management as a two-way dialogue
- providing a positive and universal framework for the description of jobs and roles
- helping to align individual and business objectives
- pointing the way to identifying, defining and building the competencies that the organisation needs its people to demonstrate.

Economic value added

The economic value added (EVA) measure represents the difference between a company's post-tax operating profit and the cost of the capital invested in the business. The cost of capital includes the cost of equity – what shareholders expect to receive through capital gains. The theory of EVA is that it is not good enough for a company simply to make a profit. It has to justify the cost of its capital, equity included. If it is not covering that, it will not make good returns for investors. Most conventional measures of company performance, such as earnings per share, ignore the cost of capital in a business.

Other economic measures of value

There is much discussion about how best to measure company performance in terms of the value created for its shareholders. This is not simply a debate about metrics theory – how companies measure value will strongly influence how they are run and will therefore affect all their performance management processes.

EVA is the current favourite, but other measures include:

- *added value* – the difference between the market value of a company's output and the costs of its inputs
- *market value added* – the difference between a company's market

capitalisation and the total capital investment; if this is positive, it will indicate the stock market wealth created

- *cash flow return on investment (CFROI)* – compares inflation-adjusted cash flows to inflation-adjusted gross revenues to find cash-flow return on investment

- *total shareholder return* – what the shareholder actually gets – ie changes in capital value plus dividends.

These measures all focus on the creation of shareholder value. They are not concerned with other aspects of corporate performance and take no account of other stakeholders.

Other more traditional financial measures include return on equity, return on capital employed, earnings per share, the price/earnings ratio, and output per employee (productivity).

PEOPLE MANAGEMENT AND ORGANISATIONAL PERFORMANCE

To date, measures of organisational value have tended to exclude or at least downplay the contribution of people. Research by the CIPD has found the phrase 'People are our most important asset' to be little more than empty rhetoric, and senior managers interviewed by Guest *et al*[2] for the report *Voices from the Boardroom* found that although most agreed with the argument that better-managed people equate to higher levels of organisational performance, few had developed strategies or measures of performance that reflected this. The evaluation and contribution of human capital to organisational performance was closely examined in Chapter 5.

Endnotes

1 Kaplan, R. S. and Norton, D. P. (1992) 'The balanced scorecard – measures that drive performance', *Harvard Business Review*, Jan–Feb, pp.71– 9.

2 Guest, D., King, Z., Conway, N., Michie, J. and Sheehan-Quinn, M. (2001) *Voices from the Boardroom*. London, CIPD.

9

Managing team performance

One of the interesting findings of our research both in 1997 and 2004 was that although everyone we contacted talked about organisational and individual performance, relatively few organisations made specific arrangements for team performance management. It seems to us that performance management for teams deserves more attention.

TEAMS AND PERFORMANCE

As Purcell *et al* (1998)[1] point out, teams can provide the

> *elusive bridge between the aims of the individual employee and the objectives of the organisation ... Teams can provide the medium for linking employee performance targets to the factors critical to the success of the business.*

This is an important aspect of performance management and provides further justification for the payment of more attention to applying it to teams.

PERFORMANCE MEASURES FOR TEAMS

Performance measures for a team will be related to the purpose of the team and its particular objectives and standards of performance. Team performance measures in this sample are therefore mainly concerned with output, activity levels (eg speed of servicing), customer service and satisfaction, and financial results. Most measures for teams, as for individuals, are likely to fall into one or more of these categories.

A distinction can be made between output/result measures of team performance and input/process measures. The output/results comprise:

- the achievement of team goals
- customer satisfaction
- quantity of work
- quality of work
- process knowledge
- maintenance of technical systems.

The input/process measures comprise:

- support of team process
- participation
- oral and written communication
- collaboration and collective effort
- conflict resolution
- planning and goal-setting
- participative decision-making
- problem-solving and analytical skills
- credibility and trust
- interdependence
- interpersonal relations
- acceptance of change
- adaptability and flexibility.

TEAM PERFORMANCE MANAGEMENT PROCESSES

Team performance management activities follow the same sequence as for individual performance management:

- agree objectives
- formulate plans to achieve objectives
- implement plans
- monitor progress
- review and assess achievement
- redefine objectives and plans in the light of the review.

The aim should be to give teams with their team leaders the maximum amount of responsibility to carry out all activities. The focus should be on self-management and self-direction.

The key activities of setting work and process objectives and conducting team reviews and individual reviews are described below.

Setting work objectives

Work objectives for a team are set in much the same way as individual objectives. They will be based on an analysis of the purpose of the team and its accountabilities for achieving results. Targets and standards of performance should be discussed and agreed by the team as a whole. These may specify what individual members are expected to contribute. Project teams will agree project plans which define what has to be done, who does it, the standards expected, and the timescale.

Setting process objectives

Process objectives are also best defined by the team getting together and agreeing how they should conduct themselves as a team under headings related to the list of team performance measures referred to above, including:

- interpersonal relationships
- the quality of participation and collaborative effort and decision-making
- the team's relationships with internal and external customers
- the capacity of the team to plan and control its activities
- the ability of the team and its members to adapt to new demands and situations
- the flexibility with which the team operates
- the effectiveness with which individual skills are used
- the quality of communications within the team and between the team and other teams or individuals.

Team performance reviews

Team performance review meetings analyse and assess feedback and control information on their joint achievements against objectives and project plans. An agenda for such meetings might be:

1   General feedback review

- progress of the team as a whole
- problems encountered by the team that have caused difficulties or hampered progress
- helps and hindrances to the operation of the team.

2   Work reviews

- how well the team has functioned
- review of the individual contribution made by each team member – ie peer review (see below)
- discussion of any new problems encountered by individual team members.

3   Group problem-solving

- analysis of reasons for any shortfalls or other problems
- agreement of what needs to be done to solve them and prevent their recurrence.

4 Update objectives

- review of new requirements, opportunities or threats
- amendment and updating of objectives and project plans.

Peer review processes can also be used in which team members assess each other under such headings as:

- overall contribution to team performance
- contribution to planning, monitoring and team review activities
- maintaining relationships with other team members and internal/external customers
- communicating
- working flexibly (taking on different roles in the team as necessary)
- co-operation with other team members.

Endnote

1 Purcell, J., Hutchinson, S. and Kinnie, N. (1998) *Getting Fit, Staying Fit: Developing lean and responsive organisations*. London, Institute of Personnel and Development.

10

360-degree feedback

360-degree feedback is an approach to assessing performance that is used to supplement or even replace the more conventional forms of assessment. In the 1997 CIPD survey, 11 per cent of the organisations used 360-degree feedback, and in 2004 this had increased slightly to 14 per cent.

Further case studies into 360-degree appraisal carried out for the CIPD in 1999 by Wendy Chivers and Philip Darling[1] found that 360-degree appraisal was mainly being used for development purposes. They also found that in many instances it was voluntary, so that individuals were able to decide whether or not they shared the feedback. This study also found that to be successful, 360-degree feedback and appraisal must be implemented in an open and trusting culture in which senior managers demonstrate active involvement and long-term commitment to the process.

In this chapter we start by defining 360-degree feedback, and describe how it is used and operated currently and whether there have been any major changes over the last few years. We then examine its advantages and disadvantages, and methods of introduction, and conclude with a summary of the outcome of our special survey carried out in 1997.

360-DEGREE FEEDBACK DEFINED

360-degree feedback is sometimes known as 'multi-source assessment'. This indicates its essential characteristic, which is that individuals are assessed under various headings by a number of different people, usually their boss and their subordinates (which is, strictly speaking, 180-degree feedback), often their colleagues and customers or clients as well (in which case it can properly be termed 360-degree feedback). Assessments are fed back to individuals in the form of ratings against a number of performance dimensions. A self-assessment process may also be incorporated using for comparison purposes the same criteria as the other generators of feedback.

Ward (1997)[2] defined 360-degree feedback as:

> the systematic collection and feedback of performance data on an individual or group derived from a number of stakeholders.

Feedback may be presented directly to individuals, or to their managers, or both. Expert counselling and coaching for individuals as a result of the feedback may be provided, often by an outside consultant.

The main driver for 360-degree feedback has been the growing complexity of organisations, which has meant that a line manager cannot necessarily appreciate all dimensions of an individual's role, or that individuals report to various points through their membership of teams or contribution to projects. It has also been implemented in some instances in an effort to create a better flow of bottom-up reporting.

THE USE OF 360-DEGREE FEEDBACK

360-degree feedback typically forms part of a self-development or management development programme. It is seldom used to generate ratings for pay purposes because most people believe that that would prejudice its developmental purpose. Many of the organisations we visited for this book were using 360-degree appraisal. Primarily, it was being used for development purposes and to align management behaviours with values and enhance leadership capability.

At First Direct, Jane Hanson told us that:

> We are rolling 360-degree appraisal out across the organisation, and it's very informal. It's not a questionnaire type of approach. It's giving people tools and techniques in a way that they can gather feedback. We encourage them so they do it on an on-going basis and don't think 'I'm just going through a process once every two years.' . . . The process is mainly about developing behaviour and skills.

At NPower, Alec Rudd, Learning and Development Manager, said that:

> We felt we needed to bring in new aspects and angles for assessment, so we introduced 360-degree feedback and self-appraisal. The philosophy behind this was that people will not change because their line manager tells them to. We wanted to create a culture to get managers to be more accountable as individuals and to enable people to be treated and think like adults. 360-degree feedback is a way to get managers to see people as they see themselves. It also includes customers.

Use for developmental purposes

360-degree appraisal tends to be used in development when:

- personal development is a priority
- performance improvement is important but is viewed as the logical outcome of a successful feedback process

- the potential for personal change and growth is emphasised rather than current performance
- strengths and weaknesses are regarded as developmental opportunities
- a long-term perspective is adopted because the ultimate goal is personal growth
- the line manager has a nominal role and may be excluded altogether
- feedback data is 'personal intelligence' and a trigger for change.

The feedback process is used in this case to help managers to formulate personal development plans or as input to a development centre.

Use for appraisal

When 360-degree feedback is used for appraisal, the focus is more on current performance. Feedback goes both to individuals and their managers, and the latter therefore play a greater part. The outcome of the feedback will be included on the agenda for performance review discussions to identify development needs and areas for improvement, and to agree on any actions required.

Use for pay

If 360-degree feedback is used for appraisal, it can easily – although controversially – be extended to inform performance-related pay decisions. Ratings are influenced by the feedback and in turn govern, or at least guide, proposals on pay increases.

Deciding on the purpose of 360-degree feedback

A number of HR specialists in the organisations we visited where 360-degree feedback was used believed strongly that it should be used only for developmental purposes. The issue then is whether the focus is on self-development or whether it is believed that development is a joint process, between managers and individuals. In the former case individuals own the feedback, whereas in the latter case it is shared.

THE RATIONALE FOR 360-DEGREE FEEDBACK

The rationale for 360-degree feedback is that:

- It recognises that a traditional top-down approach to assessment will be limited because the manager cannot appreciate fully all aspects of behaviour and performance.
- Different perspectives are brought to bear on the assessment – for example, how staff regard the leadership qualities of their managers, how colleagues perceive the ways in which individuals interact with them, and the levels of service customers (both internal and external) feel that individuals are providing.

- It creates increased self-awareness which is an important factor in developing leadership qualities.

London and Beatty (1993)[3] have suggested that the rationale for 360-degree feedback is:

- 360-degree feedback can become a powerful organisational intervention to increase awareness of the importance of aligning leader behaviour, work unit results and customer expectations, as well as increasing employee participation in leadership development and work unit effectiveness.

- 360-degree feedback recognises the complexity of management and the value of input from various sources – it is axiomatic that managers should not be assessing behaviours they cannot observe, and the leadership behaviours of subordinates may not be known to their managers.

- 360-degree feedback calls attention to important performance dimensions that may hitherto have been neglected by the organisation.

- 360-degree feedback can overcome biased appraisals because the organisation is not relying on one person's view and the inherent prejudices he or she may have.

360-DEGREE FEEDBACK – METHODOLOGY
The questionnaire

360-degree feedback processes usually obtain data by means of questionnaires which from different perspectives measure the performance or behaviours of individuals against a list of criteria, competencies or key performance requirements. Feedback is generally anonymous, but often individual can choose who they want to receive feedback from. The data is fed back to the individual either in the form of a summary or in a one-to-one discussion. One of the critical factors in the success of 360-degree feedback is that the givers of feedback are skilled in the feedback process.

Many 360-degree processes are primarily concerned to monitor competence. The competency model against which feedback is collected may be developed in-house, but there are also a number of 'off-the-shelf' products available.

The dimensions may broadly refer to leadership, management and approaches to work. The headings used in the Performance Management Group's Orbit 360-degree questionnaire are:

- Leadership
- Team player/manage people
- Self-management
- Communication
- Vision

- Organisational skills
- Decision-making
- Expertise
- Drive
- Adaptability.

The Leadership heading, for example, is defined as referring to an individual who:

Shares a clear vision and focuses on achieving it. Demonstrates commitment to the organisation's mission. Provides a coherent sense of purpose and direction, both internally and externally, harnessing energy and enthusiasm of staff.

Ratings

Ratings are given by the generators of the feedback on a scale against each heading. This may refer both to importance and performance, as in the PILAT questionnaire, which asks those completing it to rate the importance of each item on a scale of 1 (not important) to 6 (essential), and performance on a scale of 1 (weak in this area) to 6 (outstanding).

Data processing

Questionnaires are often processed with the help of software developed within the organisation or, most commonly, provided by external suppliers. This enables the data collection and analysis to be completed swiftly, with the minimum of effort and in a way that facilitates graphical as well as numerical presentation.

Graphical presentation is preferable as a means of easing the process of assimilating the data. The simplest method is to produce a profile, as illustrated in Figure 11.

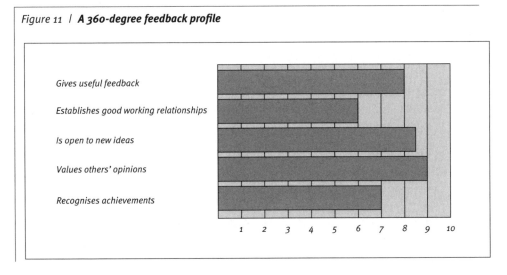

Figure 11 | *A 360-degree feedback profile*

Some of the proprietary software presents feedback data in a much more elaborate form.

Feedback

The feedback is often anonymous and may be presented to the individual (most commonly), to the individual's manager (less commonly), or to both the individual and the manager. Some organisations do not arrange for feedback to be anonymous, but whether or not feedback is anonymous depends on the organisation's culture – the more open the culture, the more likely is the source of feedback to be revealed. There could be cultural barriers to removing anonymity from feedback.

Action

The action generated by the feedback will depend on the purposes of the process – ie development, appraisal or pay. If the purpose is primarily developmental, the action may be left to individuals as part of their personal development plans, but the planning process may be shared between individuals and their managers if they both have access to the information. Even if the data only goes to the individual, it can be discussed in a performance review meeting so that joint plans can be made, and there is much to be said for adopting this approach.

DEVELOPMENT AND IMPLEMENTATION

To develop and implement 360-degree feedback, the following steps must be taken:

1 *Define objectives* – it is important to define exactly what 360-degree feedback is expected to achieve. It will be necessary to spell out the extent to which it is concerned with personal development, appraisal or pay.

2 *Decide on recipients* – who is to be at the receiving end of feedback. This may be an indication of who will eventually be covered after a pilot scheme.

3 *Decide on who will give the feedback* – the individual's manager, direct reports, team members, other colleagues, internal and external customers. A decision will also have to be made on whether HR staff or outside consultants should take part in helping managers to make use of the feedback. A further decision will need to be made on whether or not the feedback should be anonymous (it usually is).

4 *Decide how feedback will be given* – whether anonymous or not, in hard copy, or verbally.

5 *Decide on the areas of work and behaviour on which feedback will be given* – this may be in line with an existing competency model or it may take the form of a list of headings for development. Clearly, the model should fit the culture, values and type of work carried out in the organisation. But it might be decided that a list of headings or questions in a software package would be acceptable, at least to start with.

6 *Decide on the method of collecting the data* – the questionnaire could be designed in-house or a consultant's or software provider's questionnaire could be adopted, with the possible option of amending it later to produce better fit.

7 *Decide on data analysis and presentation* – again, the decision is on developing the software in-house or using a package. Most organisations installing 360-degree feedback do, in fact, purchase a package from a consultancy or software house. But the aim should be to keep it as simple as possible.

8 *Decide how the data will be used* – for what purposes and by whom. If individuals are to have faith in 360-degree feedback, there must be a clear policy about what the data is to be used for, and this must adhered to.

9 *Plan the initial implementation programme* – it is desirable to pilot the process, preferably at top level or with all the managers in a function or department. The pilot scheme should be launched with communications to those involved about the purpose of 360-degree feedback, how it will work, and the part they will play. The aim is to spell out the benefits and, as far as possible, allay any fears. Training in giving and receiving feedback will also be necessary.

10 *Analyse the outcome of the pilot scheme* – the reactions of those taking part in a pilot scheme should be analysed and necessary changes made to the process, the communication package and the training.

11 *Plan and implement the full programme* – this should include briefing, communicating, training and support from HR and, possibly, the external consultants.

12 *Monitor and evaluate* – maintain a particularly close watch on the initial implementation of feedback, but monitoring should continue. This is a process which can cause anxiety and stress, or produce little practical gain in terms of development and improved performance for a lot of effort.

The five key areas in which issues seem to arise whenever 360-degree feedback is contemplated are:

- *Fit* – does the intended use of 360-degree feedback square with the organisation's needs and culture?

- *Design* – will the process deliver the goods for its intended use, for development purposes alone or beyond?

- *Skill* – do the participants have the skills required to make 360-degree feedback work in a positive and constructive way?

- *Communication* – do staff fully understand and support the objectives of 360-degree feedback? Do they trust the process?

- *Administration* – can the growing volume of data and transactions that the processes create be handled efficiently and securely?

Chivers and Darling concluded that when organisations are implementing 360-degree feedback processes for the first time they must consider the following issues:

- To what extent does the organisation value people development in general?
- How important is feedback within the organisation?
- What is the organisation's attitude to risk-taking and failure?
- How open is senior management to the concept of 360-degree feedback?
- How would 360-degree feedback help the organisation to achieve its goals?
- How would the process fit with other HR and performance management systems?
- What processes would be put in place to promote training and support feedback-givers and -receivers?

360-DEGREE FEEDBACK – ADVANTAGES AND DISADVANTAGES
Advantages

- Individuals get a broader perspective of how they are perceived by others than previously possible.
- Individuals are more aware of their strengths and weaknesses in terms of competencies such as leadership and teamwork.
- More reliable feedback is provided for managers about their performance.
- Individuals are provided with new insights about their performance as a result of open feedback.
- Critical performance and competency requirements are clarified for employees.
- People are given a more rounded view of their performance.
- Key development areas for individuals are identified.
- Managers are more aware of how they impact upon others.

Possible problems

- people not giving frank or honest feedback
- people being put under stress in receiving or giving feedback
- lack of action following feedback
- over-reliance on technology
- too much bureaucracy.

These can all be minimised, if not avoided completely, by careful design, communication, training and follow-up.

360-DEGREE FEEDBACK – CRITERIA FOR SUCCESS

360-degree feedback is most likely to be successful when:

- it has the active support of top management who themselves take part in giving and receiving feedback and encourage everyone else to do the same
- there is commitment everywhere else to the process based on briefing, training and an understanding of the benefits to individuals as well as the organisation
- there is real determination by all concerned to use feedback data as the basis for development
- questionnaire items fit or reflect typical and significant aspects of behaviour
- items covered in the questionnaire can be related to actual events experienced by the individual
- comprehensive and well-delivered communication and training programmes are followed
- no one feels threatened by the process – this is usually often achieved by making feedback anonymous and/or getting a third-party facilitator to deliver the feedback
- feedback questionnaires are relatively easy to complete (not unduly complex or lengthy, with clear instructions)
- bureaucracy is minimised.

Endnotes

1 Chivers, W. and Darling, P. (1999) *360-degree Feedback and Organisational Culture*. London, Institute of Personnel and Development.
2 Ward, P. (1997) *360-degree Feedback*. London, Institute of Personnel and Development.
3 London, M. and Beatty, R. W. (1993) '360-degree feedback as competitive advantage', *Human Resource Management*, Summer/Fall, pp.353–72.

11

Managing under-performers

Although performance management is essentially a positive process that helps people to build on success, it has also to deal with situations in which performance is not at the expected level. The performance management sequence of planning, monitoring and review provides the ideal framework for managing performance generally and for dealing with poor performance when it occurs. In this chapter we examine initially the reasons for poor performance. We next describe what managers can do to encourage good performance, and then how they can deal with under-performers generally or during formal performance reviews. Finally, we examine the part that discipline and capability procedures play in managing performance if all else fails.

THE REASONS FOR POOR PERFORMANCE

Individuals may perform badly because of lack of ability or insufficient motivation. But as William Deming (1986)[1] pointed out, poor performance may not be their fault. It could arise from a defective system of work, inadequate leadership or guidance, the allocation of inappropriate tasks, placement in jobs that are beyond their capabilities or insufficient training.

Managers can play a major and positive part in reducing the risk of performance problems by:

- exercising effective leadership – motivating people, spelling out expectations, encouraging good teamwork

- developing systems of work that do not place impossible demands on people

- allocating work to people which is within their capacity, subject possibly to additional training. 'Stretch' objectives may reasonably be set, but they have to be achievable, although not necessarily easily

- acting as coaches – developing the talents of their staff and recognising that every occasion when they give someone an instruction or discuss work that has been completed provides an opportunity for learning. This involves providing guidance on how to carry out unfamiliar tasks or discussing the lessons learned from successful or unsuccessful accomplishment so that in the former case they can do even better in the future, and in the latter they can avoid repeating the mistake

- using performance management processes to help with all the above activities.

However, managers must recognise that it is their job to deal with under-performers along the lines described below. This takes skill and, often, courage.

DEALING WITH UNDER-PERFORMERS

To deal with poor performance it is necessary to establish that there is a problem, diagnose its cause, and decide on what needs to be done by the manager or the individual to overcome the problem. This approach can be carried out in the following five steps:

1 *Identify and agree the problem.* Analyse the feedback and, as far as possible, obtain agreement from the individual on what the shortfall has been. Feedback may be provided by managers – but it can in a sense be built into the job. This takes place when individuals are aware of their targets and standards, know what performance measures will be used and either receive feedback/control information automatically or have easy access to it. They will then be in a position to measure and assess their own performance and, if they are well-motivated and well-trained, take their own corrective actions. In other words, a self-regulating feedback mechanism exists. This is a situation which managers should endeavour to create on the grounds that prevention is better than cure.

2 *Establish the reason(s) for the shortfall.* When seeking the reasons for any shortfalls the manager should not crudely be trying to attach blame. The aim should be for the manager and the individual jointly to identify the facts that have contributed to the problem. It is on the basis of this factual analysis that decisions can be made on what to do about it by the individual, the manager, or the two of them working together.

It is necessary first to identify any causes that are outside the control of the individual. These would include external pressures, changes in requirements, systems faults, inadequate resources (time, finance, equipment), jobs or tasks allocated to people who do not have the necessary experience or attributes, inadequate induction and continuation training and poor leadership, guidance or support from the manager, team leader or colleagues. Any factors that are within the control of the individual and/or the manager can then be considered. What must be determined is the extent to which the reason for the problem is that the individual:

- has not received adequate support or guidance from the manager

- has not fully understood what he or she was expected to do
- could not do it – ability
- did not know how to do it – skill
- would not do it – attitude.

3 *Decide and agree on the action required.* Action may be taken by the individual, the manager, or both parties. This could include any of the following actions:

- Take steps to improve skills – joint action by the manager and the individual.

- Change behaviour – this is up to individuals as long as they accept that their behaviour has to change. The challenge for managers is that people will not change their behaviour simply because they are told to do so. They can only be helped to understand that certain changes to their behaviour could be beneficial not only to the organisation but also to themselves.

- Change attitudes – changing behaviour is easier than changing attitudes, which may be deep-rooted; the sequence is therefore to change behaviour first, so far as this is possible, and allow attitude changes to follow.

- Provide more support or guidance from the manager.

- Clarify expectations jointly.

- Develop abilities and skills – defining the steps that individuals may be expected to take steps to develop themselves but also indicating how the manager can provide help in the form of coaching, additional experience or training.

- Redesign the job.

Whatever action is agreed, both parties must understand how they will know that it has succeeded. Feedback arrangements can be made, but individuals should be encouraged to monitor their own performance and take further action as required.

4 *Resource the action.* Provide the coaching, training, guidance, experience or facilities required to enable the agreed actions to happen.

5 *Monitor and provide feedback.* Both managers and individuals monitor performance, ensure that feedback is provided or obtained and analysed, and agree on any further actions that may be necessary.

HANDLING PERFORMANCE PROBLEMS AT REVIEW MEETINGS

Although the management of performance is a continuous process, formal performance reviews clearly provide a good opportunity to analyse and to reflect on performance problems and to agree solutions. These discussions will be based on feedback which involves providing constructive criticism or self-assessment.

Criticising constructively is not something that all managers like doing or do well. Fletcher (1993)[2] believes that

> *when tackling performance weaknesses you should remember that they may be aspects of a person's performance that are only weak in comparison with that individual's overall performance and not weak in comparison with other people. If this is the case, you should point it out to the appraisee saying, in effect, that your aim is to help the good to become better.*

He has suggested the following methods of handling criticism:

- Let reviewees know that their frankness in identifying any shortcomings is appreciated.

- Get reviewees to produce their own ideas on remedial action.

- Provide reviewees with reassurance if they mention an aspect of their performance which falls below their own standards but you think is satisfactory.

- If reviewees do not agree that there is a problem, be firm but specific, giving examples.

- Confine comments to weaknesses that can be put right: do not try to alter the reviewee's personality.

- Do not tackle more than two weaknesses in one meeting – there is a limit to how much criticism individuals can take without becoming defensive.

THE USE OF A CAPABILITY PROCEDURE

The positive approach to solving under-performance is by joint analysis and problem-solving, and by counselling. If these and the other ways of managing performance mentioned earlier in this chapter do not produce the desired improvements, it may be necessary to leave the performance management process and invoke a capability procedure.

Capability procedures exist to deal specifically with performance problems, leaving other disciplinary matters such as absenteeism to be dealt with through a disciplinary procedure. The following is an example of an organisation's capability procedure.

Capability procedure

Policy

The company aims are to ensure that performance expectations and standards are defined, performance is monitored and employees are given appropriate feedback, training and support to meet these standards.

Procedure

1   If a manager/project leader believes that an employee's performance is not up to standard, an informal discussion will be held with the employee to try to establish the reason and agree on the actions required by the employee to meet the standard over a defined period. As necessary, the manager/team leader will explain the standards and what is expected from the employee. Coaching and other support will be offered as required. If it is agreed that the established standards are not reasonably attainable, they will be reviewed.

2   If it is established that the performance problems are related to the employee's personal life, the necessary counselling/support will be provided.

3   If it is decided that the poor performance emanates from a change in the organisation's standards, those standards will be explained to the employee and help will be offered to obtain conformity with the standards.

4   If it is apparent that the poor performance constitutes misconduct, the disciplinary procedure will be invoked.

5   Should the employee show no (or insufficient) improvement over a defined period (weeks/months), a formal interview will be arranged between the employee (together with a representative if so desired). The aims of this interview will be to:

- explain clearly the shortfall between the employee's performance and the required standard
- identify the cause(s) of the unsatisfactory performance and to determine what – if any – remedial treatment (eg training, retraining, support, etc) can be given
- obtain the employee's commitment to reaching that standard
- set a reasonable period for the employee to reach the standard and agree on a monitoring system during that period, and
- tell the employee what will happen if that standard is not met.

The outcome of this interview will be recorded in writing and a copy will be given to the employee.

6 At the end of the review period a further formal interview will be held, at which time:

- if the required improvement has been made, the employee will be told of this and encouraged to maintain the improvement

- if some improvement has been made but the standard has not yet been met, the review period will be extended

- if there has been no discernible improvement, it will be indicated to the employee that he or she has failed to improve. Consideration will be given to whether there are alternative vacancies which the employee would be competent to fill. If there are, the employee will be given the option of accepting such a vacancy or being dismissed

- if such vacancies are available, the employee will be given full details of them, in writing, before being required to make a decision.

7 If all the above fails to result in a satisfactory level of performance, the disciplinary procedure will be invoked.

Endnotes

1 Deming, W. E. (1986) *Out of the Crisis*. Cambridge, Mass., Massachusetts Institute of Technology, Center for Advanced Engineering Studies.
2 Fletcher, C. (1993) *Appraisal: Routes to Improved performance*. London, Institute of Personnel and Development.

12

Developing performance management

DEVELOPING PERFORMANCE MANAGEMENT

The nine stages of a development programme are described below. At each stage it is necessary to seek the views and approval of senior management and to involve line managers, staff and their representatives in the programme. Steps will also have to be taken to communicate to staff the aims of the programme, how these aims will be met, and how the staff will be affected, emphasising the benefits to them as well as to the organisation.

Stage 1: Diagnostic review

This should establish the extent to which the following requirements are met by the existing arrangements:

- Performance management processes fit the culture of the organisation, the context in which it operates and the characteristics of its people and work practices.
- There is full support from top management.
- Performance management processes are accepted by all concerned as being natural components of good management and work practices.
- Line managers are committed to performance management.
- Line managers have the skills to carry out their performance management responsibilities effectively.
- Staff believe that performance management is carried out by their managers effectively.
- Staff believe that they benefit from performance management in the sense that they get good feedback and guidance and support in developing their talents and careers.
- Performance management processes are integrated with strategic and business planning processes.

- Performance management processes are integrated with other HR processes.

- Performance management processes help to integrate organisational, team and individual objectives.

- Performance management processes help to align organisational and individual goals, but this is not a matter of a top-down cascade of objectives. Individuals and teams are given the opportunity to put forward their views on what they can achieve and their views are listened to.

- Performance management processes recognise that there is a community of interests in the organisation and respect individual needs.

- All stakeholders within the organisation are involved in the design, development and introduction of performance management. These comprise top management, line managers, team leaders, individual employees and trade union or employee representatives.

- Performance management processes are transparent and operate fairly and equitably.

- Managers and team leaders take action to ensure that there is a shared understanding generally of the vision, strategy, goals and values of the organisation.

- Performance management processes are used by managers and team leaders to help people feel that they are valued by the organisation.

- The focus of performance management is demonstrably on the development of people. Financial rewards are a secondary consideration if, indeed, they are associated with performance management.

- There are competence frameworks in place, and these have been developed specially for the organisation with the full involvement of all concerned.

- The aims and operation of performance management and how it can benefit all concerned are communicated thoroughly and effectively.

- Training in performance management skills is given to managers, team leaders *and* employees generally.

Stage 2: Planning

Planning the development and introduction of performance management requires:

- the preparation of a summary of the diagnostic review, setting out an analysis of the situation, the identification of reasons for change and the general approach that should be adopted to the development of new or improved performance management processes

- a definition of the objectives that the new arrangements are intended to achieve, covering such areas as performance improvement through the creation of a performance culture, upholding core values, developing skills, competencies and potential, supporting talent management and providing a basis for contingent pay decisions

- an assessment of the resources required to develop performance management
- an assessment of the costs and benefits of the proposed development
- an overall assessment of the approach to performance management and how it should be introduced and maintained

One HR director informed us that when he was considering the development of performance management, they

took a conscious decision not to have a formal policy as we are trying to get away from policies and procedures unless they are really needed.

Stage 3: Programming

The programme should set out a timetable for achieving the aims agreed at the planning stage covering the various processes of performance management (planning, review and assessment) and in more detail the arrangements for:

- obtaining senior management approval and support
- involving line managers and defining their requirements from performance management, taking particular account of the need to get them to buy into the scheme
- involving staff and their representatives in the design of the scheme to ensure that they own it
- training managers and staff both in the skills associated with performance management (how) and the rationale for performance management (why)
- obtaining the resources required to develop the scheme (people and money)
- pilot testing the proposed scheme
- setting the timetable for development and introduction
- communicating details of the plan and the scheme to employees (it is vital that this should be done thoroughly and in good time)
- establishing success criteria
- monitoring and evaluating implementation, including timescales.

Stage 4: Scheme design

The following points should be considered when designing the performance management scheme and deciding on the processes required:

- the aims and purpose of performance management, how it will benefit all concerned and how these aims can be achieved

- the different needs and perceptions of different stakeholder groups

- the use of objectives – the form they should take, how they will be measured

- how individual objectives will be aligned to corporate objectives

- how objectives will be agreed

- how performance planning should take place

- the use of personal development plans

- approaches to managing performance on a continuous basis

- how and when performance management review meetings should take place, including a description of the approach that should be used to ensure that a genuine dialogue takes place and a definition of responsibilities of both parties for preparing for the review as well as taking part in it

- the documentation required – ensuring that it is simple and easy to use

- the uses to which performance data may be put, including its contribution to human capital evaluation or management information systems such as 'dashboards'

- the link to performance- or contribution-related pay, if any – how assessments will inform pay decisions

- what form of rating, if any, should be used

- if rating is used, methods of achieving fairness and consistency

- the use of 360-degree appraisal

- the use of self-appraisal, peer appraisal or team appraisal

- a definition of the skills managers must use and how they should be developed (see below)

- a description of how performance management fits with other people management and development initiatives such as career management, talent management or succession planning

- a plan for gaining the commitment of line managers and employees generally to performance management

- a plan for maintaining performance management after it has been introduced.

Stage 5: Pilot test

It is very desirable to pilot test the proposed performance management arrangements, possibly in one part of the organisation. Ideally, the test should extend over a full year of operation and cover drawing up performance agreements, objective-setting, performance reviews, the preparation of personal development plans and documentation. The aims of the test should be defined and the criteria used for assessing test results in each of these areas should be predetermined.

Stage 6: Briefing

An overall description of the performance management scheme should be issued to all employees that sets out its objectives and method of operation and the benefits it is expected to provide for all concerned. Some organisations have prepared elaborate and lengthy briefing documents, but fairly succinct documents often suffice as long as they are written in simple language and are well produced.

It is desirable to supplement written with oral briefings through a briefing group system, if there is one, or a special briefing programme. In a large or dispersed organisation this briefing will have to be carried out by line managers who will have to be briefed themselves on what they should do.

Stage 7: Training

Performance management is not easy. It requires high levels of skill by everyone involved and the skills are likely to be ones that have not yet been developed or put into practice. For example, providing feedback that will motivate and help to develop people is not easy for those who have not done it before. Receiving, responding to and acting on feedback are similarly unfamiliar skills for many people. The agreement of objectives and competence requirements, the application of performance measures and methods of analysing and using the outcomes of reviews may also be strange. The concepts of personal development planning and self-managed learning will be new to many people.

The main performance management skills that people have to learn are:

- defining accountabilities and key result areas
- defining objectives
- identifying and using performance measures
- defining and assessing competencies and behavioural requirements
- giving and receiving feedback
- questioning and listening
- identifying development needs and preparing and implementing personal development plans
- diagnosing and solving performance problems
- coaching.

Training may be provided by formal courses, but there will be a limit to the amount of time that can be spared. Continuing encouragement, coaching, guidance and support is also required. This can be provided by HR but it can profitably be supplemented by the use of experienced line managers as coaches.

The importance of training was stressed by one of our interviewees:

> *People have to see the benefits of performance management, and I think training is the key thing – people almost measure themselves on how much training they have received. This is what makes it a key focus for us.*

Jane Hanson at First Direct told us about their approach to training:

> *We've just revamped the performance management training into three modules. The first two are specifically designed for new team leaders, or somebody new to line management. They cover the basics of performance management. Module one was developed around the performance cycle – the plan, support, monitor and review cycle. We talk to them about dealing with poor performers, how they reward and recognise their good performers, and how they balance their time so they are not spending 40 per cent of their time with the 20 per cent who are not performing. We explain the different tools and techniques available to them to manage their people effectively.*

> *Module two is more complex as this covers potential issues with people: how they manage those issues, what they need to do – for example, fact-finding to find out more about what is happening. We deal with the disciplinary framework ultimately as well.*

> *Module three is designed for our more experienced managers: the people who are involved in really intensive coaching and supporting staff. It covers what happens if they have got it wrong – what are the implications for the business? What do we need to do when we move into the disciplinary arena because what we've done so far has not been effective?*

> *The three modules are there to support the managers as they develop and get more involved in the complex issues surrounding the development of individuals and as they manage their performance all the way through. We also cover their own development – thinking about their future roles.*

> *We don't actually run a specific course for individuals on how to conduct a performance appraisal, but the message we give to team leaders and managers is that if this is new to the individual and this is their first appraisal, you need to sit down with them, go though the documentation, and explain what you expect from them when they come to have the meeting. We emphasise that it is a two-way process, explaining that individuals should contribute to the discussion, because it's not just about the manager's view – it's about their view as well.*

Stage 8: Maintenance

Performance management processes have to be nurtured. The fundamental mistake many organisations have made is to believe that all they have to do is to design an elegant system complete with documentation, to a flourish of trumpets introduce the system with the help of a glossy brochure, run one or two half-day training courses, and it will all happen as planned. But it will not. Plans have to be prepared and implemented that provide for line managers to be encouraged on a continuing basis to carry out their performance management responsibilities properly and be given any support or guidance they may need to do so. Employees generally should also be encouraged to play their part and be provided with support. The systematic monitoring and evaluation of performance management as described below is essential to generate the information required to maintain it as an effective process.

One of our interviewees explained their approach to the maintenance of performance management:

> *We have a process and we encourage people to follow it. We tell managers that 'If you have not done it at the end of the year, you still need to decide on a salary increase,' so that is a big driver. We do everything to remind people. We use screen savers that say 'Have you completed the process?' and we chase people to tell them that 'If you have no performance management agreement by the end of the year, you won't get a salary increase.' There's a help button on the intranet site, along with a help phone number and a help email address.*

> *We produce line manager briefing packs. We have a performance management training programme about the philosophy of performance management which most of our managers have gone through. There is an intranet site linked to our HR help desk that takes them through the process with tips and tools. This year we are working with the executive leader team looking at 'how to do it'. It's pretty comprehensive. We also have a masterclass for senior people. And we are investigating the use of e-learning.*

Stage 9: Evaluation

It is essential to monitor the effectiveness of performance management to evaluate its effectiveness, ideally once a year. Engelmann and Roesch[1] have suggested that the following areas should be examined when evaluating a 'performance system':

- how well it supports the organisation's objectives
- how it is linked to the organisation's critical success factors
- how well it defines and establishes individual objectives
- how well it relates to job responsibilities and performance expectations
- how effectively it encourages personal development
- how easy (or difficult) it is to use
- how objective or subjective, clear or ambiguous evaluation criteria are
- whether it addresses company policies and procedures
- whether it is fairly and consistently administered
- how well supervisors and employees are trained to use and live under the system
- how it is linked to pay.

In the Scottish Parliament the definition of what constitutes good performance management provides a basis for evaluating it:

- New staff know what is expected of them from the outset.
- Everyone is clear about corporate goals and works towards them.
- Objectives are SMART (Specific, Measurable, Achievable, Relevant, Time-related).
- A system exists to accommodate day-to-day performance feedback.
- Evidence is available to support assessments.
- The Personal Development Plan is used formally to help self-developmental activities and/or improve performance.
- The line manager provides and the jobholder undertakes the training needed to support the individual and the organisation.
- Appropriate support is in place to eliminate poor performance.

Evaluation of the process of performance management can take place by conducting opinion surveys or asking individuals to complete a questionnaire immediately following a review meeting. The survey or questionnaire could ask them to give their reactions (eg fully agree, partly agree, partly disagree, fully disagree) to the following statements:

- I was given plenty of opportunity to contribute to formulating my objectives.
- I am quite satisfied that the objectives I agreed to were fair.
- I felt that the meeting to agree objectives helped me to focus on what I should be aiming to achieve.
- I received good feedback from my manager during the year on how well I was doing.
- My manager was always prepared to provide guidance when I ran into any problems with my work.
- The performance review was conducted by my manager in a friendly and helpful way.
- My manager fully recognised my achievements during the year.
- If any criticisms were made during the review, they were based on fact, not on opinion.
- I was given plenty of opportunity by my manager to discuss the reasons for any problems with my work.
- I felt that generally the comments made by my manager at the review meeting were fair.

- The review meeting ended with a clear plan of action for the future with which I agreed.

- I felt well-motivated after the meeting.

DEVELOPING THE COMMITMENT AND CAPABILITY OF LINE MANAGERS

The key factor in developing a successful process of performance management is to gain the commitment of line managers and to ensure that they are capable of managing performance effectively. Of course, it is important also to develop appropriate processes, to convince employees that they will benefit from performance management and to provide them with training. But as Hutchinson and Purcell 2003[2] emphasise, it is line managers who bring policies to life. They found that individuals' relationships with their line managers significantly influenced their attitude to performance management. In short, good line managers can make even the worst performance management process work for them because they will adapt it to do what they know they have to do. Poor line managers will struggle with even the most carefully crafted and designed process. The key to successful performance management is not just about getting management buy-in, although that is vital – it is about developing people management capability in line managers to ensure that they really do bring the policy to life and use it to engender commitment and ultimately better performance from the individuals they manage. Hutchinson and Purcell conclude:

> *A generation ago it was common to talk about the 'forgotton supervisors', the layer of staff who are not really managers, no longer workers but stuck in the middle and often neglected. Much has changed since then in many organisations – but there is still much to be done to give front line managers the attention, the respect, the training and the policy tools they need to deliver, through people management, better employment relations and higher performance.*

Successful performance management rests not just with HR and senior management but also with front line managers, and it is vital that they receive the training and support they need to make it happen.

Endnotes

1 Engelmann, C. H. and Roesch, C. H. (1996) *Managing Individual Performance.* Scottsdale, Ariz., American Compensation Association.
2 Hutchinson, S. and Purcell, J. (2003) *Bringing Policies to Life: The vital role of front line managers in people management.* London, CIPD.

Appendix A

An example of a competency framework

The areas of competency incorporated in this framework are:

- Manage performance
- Manage oneself
- Manage others
- Manage relationships
- Manage communications
- Manage customer service
- Manage continuous improvement
- Manage resources.

For each competency there are definitions of the six levels at which they are present in the organisation. The competencies are cumulative so that anyone at level 6 should have the competencies defined at that level and also the competencies at the five lower levels.

Behavioural indicators are also given for each competency level. These are simply examples – they are not meant to be exhaustive. Again, they are cumulative, although in this case higher-level examples could often be relevant at lower levels.

Manage performance

Do things well and achieve the objectives and standards agreed for the role

Levels	1	2	3	4	5	6
Behavioural indicators	• Focus on what needs to be done • Meet service and quality standards • Act in line with specific directions	• Propose targets and standards for role • Plan day-to-day activities • Work under fairly close supervision	• Determine and work to demanding goals • Take initiative to solve problems • Work with only general supervision	• Set challenging goals • Create measures of achievement • Schedule complex work	• Set challenging goals for the team • Meet expectations through the team • Deal with often conflicting priorities	• Commit significant resources to meet challenging goals • Plan strategically • Make strategic decisions
Positive indicators	• Carries out work as required • Completes work on time • Meets quality/service standards	• Sees things through • Asks for ground rules • Is committed to achieving high-quality results	• Shows commitment to make it happen • Seeks to raise quality standards • Puts measures in place	• Actions match words • Takes ownership of things to be done • Evaluates and revises deadlines as necessary	• Takes responsibility for outcomes • Always has a follow-up course of action • Makes contingency plans	• Does everything within his/her means to ensure that things get done to the best of his/her ability • Confronts issues
Negative indicators	• Does not follow instructions • Is often late in delivering expected results • Work not up to standard	• Frequently forgets things • Has to be chased to meet deadlines • Is not concerned with quality	• Doesn't commit to action • Sometimes misses deadlines • Is complacent about quality	• Does minimum he/she can get away with • Relies on others to complete actions • Has no pride in the job	• Blames others for personal failure • Conceals situations when things go wrong • Focuses on less important activities	• Builds achievements to be greater than they are • Agrees unrealistic deadlines • Prioritises badly

Manage oneself

Make decisions, solve problems, take initiative, manage time, improve own performance, work to support The Children's Trust's values and goals

Levels	1	2	3	4	5	6
Behavioural indicators	• Take steps to improve performance • Manage own time to complete work • Be aware of Trust values	• Make decisions confidently • Manage own learning • Take pride in achieving results	• Generate practical solutions • Promote Trust's image and values • Confidently apply knowledge and skills	• Understand complex situations in order to develop action plans • Have complete confidence in own ability	• Understand key issues affecting the Trust • Accept challenge and demanding assignments	• Understand in depth the Trust's values and goals. • Welcome highly challenging situations
Positive indicators	• Gets on with work without supervision • Demonstrates a willingness to learn • Acts in line with Trust's values	• Takes initiative to solve problems • Seeks opportunities for learning • Schedules and uses time effectively	• Quickly identifies the right thing to do • Continuously develops expertise • Actively promotes Trust's values	• Acts decisively, taking a broad view • States problems clearly • Evaluates conflicting priorities	• Reaches clear conclusions based on understanding of underlying issues • Deals with crisis situations effectively	• Demonstrates understanding of critical issues • Makes good-quality strategic decisions
Negative indicators	• Needs constant supervision • Shows no interest in learning • Is unaware of values	• Is unwilling to act on own initiative • Takes no steps to improve performance	• Makes snap decisions with little foundation • Does not keep skills and knowledge up to date	• Is indecisive, takes a superficial and narrow view • Off-loads decisions to others	• Focuses on symptoms, not causes • Cannot cope with pressurised situations	• Fails to make timely decisions • Does not consider long-term impact of decisions

Manage others

Get results through people; exercise leadership; develop staff

Levels	1	2	3	4	5	6
Behavioural indicators	• Act appropriately as a team member, responding well to leadership	• Take a leadership role within team when appropriate	• Provide leadership as appropriate, setting the example and giving direction and support	• Give clear direction and guidance • Motivate and coach team members • Monitor and review performance	• Get the team to accept and achieve challenging goals • Promote the development of team members	• Provide visionary and inspirational leadership • Encourage the development of staff at all levels
Positive indicators	• Co-operates well with team leader and colleagues • Responds positively to suggestions and feedback	• Rises to the occasion when leadership required • Is accepted in leadership role by team members	• Agrees clear team goals • Inspires team to achieve goals • Leads by example	• Gives clear direction • Offers firm support and guidance • Knows what's going on and takes swift corrective action	• Encourages team members to take joint responsibility for their achievements • Lets people know that they are valued	• Encourages open, honest and constructive behaviour that helps the team to find its way
Negative indicators	• Is not a team player; disruptive • Is unwilling to work towards team goals • Ignores feedback	• Is reluctant to take on responsibility for team performance • Cannot win respect of team members	• Doesn't explain why things need to be done • Fails to clarify team goals and standards	• Fails to allocate tasks appropriately • Ignores contribution of individuals • Lets things slide	• Imposes own views on team • Operates a 'blame culture' • Takes no interest in developing people	• Is unable to create a shared vision for team • Adopts a 'command and control' approach

Manage relationships

Exert influence; build and maintain effective relationships with colleagues and stakeholders; participate in or run meetings

Levels	1	2	3	4	5	6
Behavioural indicators	• Maintain friendly, helpful and supportive relationships with immediate colleagues and customers • Participate well in team activities	• Relate well to internal and external customers and colleagues • Take active part in team meetings	• Exert influence on day-to-day matters with colleagues • Build effective networks with colleagues and stakeholders • Lead small departmental meetings	• Exert influence on people to take action in ways that will make a positive although short-term impact on the performance of the function/department • Lead large functional or departmental meetings	• Exert influence on people to take action in ways which will make a long-term impact on the performance of the function/department • Lead large functional or departmental meetings	• Exert influence on people to take action in ways which will make a long-term impact on the performance of the function/department • Lead large functional or departmental meetings
Positive indicators	• Gets on well with colleagues and customers • Takes part in team activities; is fully accepted by team colleagues • Views others positively	• Builds good relationships with internal and external customers • Gets on well with people • Shows tact, sensitivity and support	• Offers support through regular contact; makes time for people • Offers ideas, suggestions and advice relevant to the needs of the individual • Expresses point of view clearly in order to reach agreement	• Expresses views and proposals persuasively • Is sensitive to other people's needs and wants and adjusts proposals and recommendations accordingly • Listens, reflects and checks own understanding	• Presents proposals which are logical, practical and persuasive • Has contacts spread throughout the organisation and with key external people • Looks for shared ways to get round problems and disagreements	• Marshals powerful and compelling arguments which clearly address the issue and are developed logically from the facts • Networks widely to get a strategic overview • Works to achieve consensus, rather than force own direction • Is seen and used as an important contact by key people inside and outside the Trust
Negative indicators	• Courtesy depends on mood • Is often difficult to deal with • Does not contribute much to team activities	• Is unresponsive to others' contributions, feelings and concerns • Is tactless, says things without considering effect • Takes no real interest in the concerns of others	• Misunderstands how others feel • Pursues own agenda, irrespective of others • Does not listen to or encourage contributions from others	• Produces an unconvincing case or weak arguments when making a proposal or suggestion • Fails to build up or maintain good relationships • Doesn't treat people as equals	• Arguments supporting proposals are not thought through and do not hang together • Finds it difficult to get others to accept complex or controversial proposals • Makes little attempt to network with other people, inside or outside the Trust	• Proposals are ill-prepared and lack conviction • Proposals fail to address the issues which concern recipients • Goes own way, irrespective of the needs of other people

Manage communications

Communicate orally or in writing to colleagues, customers/clients and external individuals or organisations

Levels	1	2	3	4	5	6
Behavioural indicators	• Communicate orally to colleagues or customers in own area on day-to-day matters	• Communicate orally or in writing to colleagues or customers in other parts of the organisation or externally on day-to-day matters	• Communicate orally or in writing to colleagues, customers or external individuals/organisations on matters of longer-term significance	• Communicate orally or in writing on significant departmental or functional matters	• Communicate orally and in writing on complex or sensitive issues to inform colleagues and stakeholders on matters affecting the function	• Convey highly complex and sensitive information in order to bring about changes or inform stakeholders on matters which have a major impact on the Trust
Positive indicators	• Makes himself/herself understood	• Speaks clearly and audibly and gains the attention of those he/she is talking to • Written information is presented clearly • Uses language that other people can understand	• Speaks persuasively and with conviction • Delivers concise communications that are readily understood, simple to interpret and avoid jargon	• Actively listens • Acknowledges other people's feelings and emotions • Tailors message to recipient	• Expresses ideas lucidly and presents arguments in a logical manner • Written communications are easy to follow, well laid out and have an internal logic	• Speaks persuasively and with conviction • Gains the complete attention of those to whom he/she is speaking • Letters, memoranda and reports are concise, lucid and to the point • Selects most appropriate means of communication
Negative indicators	• Fails to get message across	• Uses language poorly • Does not readily communicate, share with others	• Communications are vague and irrelevant • Letters or memoranda are badly constructed and written	• Sends lengthy, verbose, ambiguous messages • Tends to waffle	• Uses language poorly and expresses ideas in a woolly manner • Reports and memoranda are poorly laid out and difficult to follow	• Reports, memoranda and presentations lack structure and are unclear • Conclusions are not well justified

Manage customer service

Provide high levels of service for internal and external customers/clients in accordance with exacting standards

Levels	1	2	3	4	5
Behavioural indicators	• Provide services for internal and external customers	• Build and maintain good relationships with customers	• Contribute to the development and maintenance of high standards of customer service	• Contribute to the development of customer service standards in the function or department and play an active part in achieving them	• Contribute to the development of customer service standards in the function or department and play an active part in achieving them
Positive indicators	• Meets expressed needs of internal customers	• Handles customer's queries effectively and knows where to channel queries within the organisation • Understands customer problems	• Identifies potential opportunities to help customers • Asks customers how services could be improved	• Builds collaborative relationships with customers • Establishes high level of trust among customers as witnessed by customer feedback	• Develops extensive customer networks • Sets standards of customer serviced and ensures that they are met
Negative indicators	• Has no appreciation of customer needs or pressures • Doesn't listen to customers	• Is unaware of customer needs • Passes enquiries when he/she could have taken action himself/herself	• Fails to respond to customer requests or queries • Does not deliver standard of service customers have the right to expect	• Customer enquiries and complaints are not attended to swiftly • Gets negative feedback from customers	• Is too little concerned with setting and monitoring customer service standards

Manage continuous improvement

Constantly seek ways of improving the quality of services, the relevance and appeal of those services to the needs of customer/clients, and the effectiveness of support and operational systems

Levels	1	2	3	4	5	6
Behavioural indicators	• Improve work methods to achieve higher levels of efficiency • Ensure that quality considerations are given proper attention	• Identify areas for improvement and take action to achieve improvement plans • Give close and continuous attention to the delivery of high-quality services	• Set targets for improvement • Develop and implement programmes for implementing change • Contribute to the development of quality assurance and control processes and ensure that they are implemented	• Develop and oversee the implementation of quality assurance and control processes • Develop and monitor continuous improvement programmes and stimulate action as required • Take part in the management of change	• Develop a culture which encourages innovation and continuous improvement • Manage major change programmes in area of responsibility	• Develop a culture which encourages innovation and continuous improvement • Manage major change programmes in area of responsibility
Positive indicators	• Makes suggestions to manager on better ways of carrying out work	• Is prepared to try doing things differently • Is aware of quality standards and takes steps to improve service delivery	• Encourages the development of new ideas and methods, especially those concerned with the provision of quality services • Is conscious of the factors that enable change to take place smoothly	• Discusses ideas with colleagues and customers and formulates views on how to improve services and processes • Understands the need to seek ideas from outside own experience • Takes action to ensure that change is accepted and acted upon	• Continually seeks to improve • Generates different options and assesses the risks and implications of pursuing them	• Challenges perceptions and inbuilt prejudices • Is prepared to take risks, challenge rules
Negative indicators	• Is not interested in doing anything different	• Is complacent, believes that there is no room for improvement	• Doesn't try anything that hasn't been done before	• Follows previous practices without considering whether there is any need to change	• Is reluctant to admit that there is any need to change	• Accepts the status quo • Is risk-averse even in situations where some risk is inevitable if progress is to be made

Manage resources

Use resources (money, equipment, stock, space) efficiently; set and control budgets; formulate and implement plans; plan and manage projects

Levels	1	2	3	4	5	6
Behavioural indicators	• Support the efficient use of resources • Administer (where applicable) stock, equipment or petty cash	• Use resources efficiently	• Contribute to the setting of budgets • Manage budgets and allocate resources within them	• Set budget • Control budget and re-allocate resources within it as necessary • Manage projects within area of responsibility	• Contribute to the business plan within area of authority, setting out resources required • Monitor and evaluate progress • Contribute to the planning and control of cross-functional projects • Exercise overall control of resource allocation in area	• Contribute to the development of the Trust's Business Plan in area of responsibility • Ensure that the corporate plan as it affects area of responsibility is implemented • Monitor and evaluate use and allocation of key resources • Plan and oversee major Trust projects
Positive indicators	• Looks after resources carefully	• Consistently achieves a high standard with regard to the use and control of resources	• Makes sensible contributions to the budget-setting process, having regard to the way resources need to be allocated • Keeps within budget, minimising variances	• Sets realistic and acceptable budgets • Controls budgets to ensure that negative variances do not occur • Ensures that resources are used efficiently and effectively • Departmental or functional projects completed to specification, in time and within budget	• Makes a significant contribution to the planning process in area of authority with particular reference to the resources required to achieve plans • Carefully monitors activities and budgets to ensure that resources are used effectively and that there is no over-spend • Cross-functional projects completed to specification, in time and within budget	• Makes a significant contribution to the Trust's business planning process with particular reference to the resources required to achieve plans • Monitors and controls implementation of plans to ensure that their objectives are achieved • Major Trust projects completed to specification, in time and within budget
Negative indicators	• Is careless and wasteful with resources	• Pays insufficient attention to ensuring that resources are used efficiently	• Contributions to budget-setting are inadequate • Cannot keep within budget	• Budgets are unrealistic and badly controlled • Resources are not used effectively	• Plays inadequate part in planning • Has lax approach to control	• Makes poor contribution to business planning • Fails to exercise proper control

Appendix B

Performance management form

PERFORMANCE AND DEVELOPMENT AGREEMENT AND REVIEW	
Name:	Forename(s):
Job title:	Department:
Reviewer's name:	Job title:
PERFORMANCE AND DEVELOPMENT AGREEMENT	
Objectives	Performance measures
Competencies	Agreed actions

PERSONAL DEVELOPMENT PLAN		
Development need	How it is to be met	Action by whom

PERFORMANCE AND DEVELOPMENT REVIEW	
Objectives	Achievements
Competencies	Actions taken
Development needs	Actions taken

Comments by reviewer:
Signed: Date:

Comments by reviewee:
Signed: Date:

Appendix C
Survey questionnaire

SECTION A – WHAT IS PERFORMANCE MANAGEMENT?

1   **Please indicate the extent to which you agree/disagree with the following statements regardless of whether this reflects current practice in your organisation**

	Strongly agree	Slightly agree	Slightly disagree	Strongly disagree
The most important aspect of performance management is the setting of challenging and stretching goals	☐ 01	☐ 02	☐ 03	☐ 04
Performance management will inevitably become a bureaucratic chore	☐ 01	☐ 02	☐ 03	☐ 04
Performance management will only succeed if it is part of an integrated approach to the management of people	☐ 01	☐ 02	☐ 03	☐ 04
Performance management will only succeed if it integrates the goals of individuals with those of the organisation	☐ 01	☐ 02	☐ 03	☐ 04
It is essential that line managers own the performance management system	☐ 01	☐ 02	☐ 03	☐ 04
Performance-related pay is an essential part of performance management	☐ 01	☐ 02	☐ 03	☐ 04
The focus of performance management should be developmental	☐ 01	☐ 02	☐ 03	☐ 04
Performance management should be a continuous and integrated part of the employee-line manager relationship	☐ 01	☐ 02	☐ 03	☐ 04
The main objective of performance management should be to motivate individuals	☐ 01	☐ 02	☐ 03	☐ 04

	Strongly agree	Slightly agree	Slightly disagree	Strongly disagree
Performance management is an essential tool in the management of organisational culture	☐ 01	☐ 02	☐ 03	☐ 04
The effectiveness of performance management is easier to measure in qualitative rather than quantitative terms	☐ 01	☐ 02	☐ 03	☐ 04
Everyone must be trained in performance management techniques for PM system to be successful	☐ 01	☐ 02	☐ 03	☐ 04
Performance management distracts people from more important core activities	☐ 01	☐ 02	☐ 03	☐ 04
It is essential that performance management is accompanied by extensive communication to ensure its aims are fully understood	☐ 01	☐ 02	☐ 03	☐ 04
Performance management should be distanced as far as possible from payment systems	☐ 01	☐ 02	☐ 03	☐ 04
Quantifiable measures of performance are essential to successful performance management	☐ 01	☐ 02	☐ 03	☐ 04

SECTION B – ORGANISATIONAL BACKGROUND

1　**Which of the following economic sectors best describes your organisation?**

Public Sector ?　　　　　　　　　☐ 01
Private-sector manufacturing　　☐ 02
Private-sector service/voluntary　☐ 03
Other *(please specify)*　　　　　☐ 04 ....

....

2　**Approximately how many people are employed in the business establishment you are replying on behalf of?**

100-249 ☐ 01　　250-999 ☐ 02　　1000-4999 ☐ 03　　5000 plus ☐ 04

SECTION C – NATURE OF CURRENT PERFORMANCE ARRANGEMENTS

1　**Does your organisation operate formal performance-management processes?**

Yes ☐ 01　　　No ☐ 02

If yes, which of the following groups of employees do these processes apply to?

Senior Managers ☐ 01   Other managers/team leaders ☐ 02
Technical/clerical ☐ 03   Professionals ☐ 04   Manual/blue collar ☐ 05

Other *(please specify)* ☐ 06 ....

Do the performance management processes you operate differ between the above groups?

Yes ☐ 01   No ☐ 02

If yes, please complete the rest of this questionnaire only for those performance-management arrangements which apply to the largest group within your work-force, and please specify by ticking the relevant boxes below which employees are included within this largest group.

Senior Managers ☐ 01   Other managers/team leaders ☐ 02
Technical/clerical ☐ 03   Professionals ☐ 04   Manual/blue collar ☐ 05

Other *(please specify)* ☐ 06 ....

If you do not operate formal performance-management processes, have you any plans to do so within the next two years?

Yes ☐ 01   No ☐ 02

and have you had a performance-management system at any time in the last 10 years?

Yes ☐ 01   No ☐ 02

If yes, why did you abandon it?

Too costly	☐ 01
Too time-consuming	☐ 02
Lack of commitment from line managers	☐ 03
Did not achieve objectives	☐ 04
Other *(please specify)*	☐ 06 ....

Please only proceed if you do currently operate formal performance-management processes. If you do not, please return the form now in the pre-paid envelope provided.

2 **Please indicate which of the following features of performance-management processes are included in your arrangements, and how effective you believe these to be.**

	Are a feature	Very effective	Mostly effective	Partly effective	Not effective
Individual annual appraisal	☐ 01	☐ 02	☐ 03	☐ 04	☐ 05
Twice-yearly (bi-annual) appraisal	☐ 01	☐ 02	☐ 03	☐ 04	☐ 05
Rolling appraisal	☐ 01	☐ 02	☐ 03	☐ 04	☐ 05
360-degree appraisal	☐ 01	☐ 02	☐ 03	☐ 04	☐ 05
Peer appraisal	☐ 01	☐ 02	☐ 03	☐ 04	☐ 05
Self-appraisal	☐ 01	☐ 02	☐ 03	☐ 04	☐ 05
Team appraisal	☐ 01	☐ 02	☐ 03	☐ 04	☐ 05
Subordinate feedback	☐ 01	☐ 02	☐ 03	☐ 04	☐ 05
Continuous assessment	☐ 01	☐ 02	☐ 03	☐ 04	☐ 05
Competence assessment	☐ 01	☐ 02	☐ 03	☐ 04	☐ 05
Objective-setting and review	☐ 01	☐ 02	☐ 03	☐ 04	☐ 05
Performance-related pay	☐ 01	☐ 02	☐ 03	☐ 04	☐ 05
Competence-related pay	☐ 01	☐ 02	☐ 03	☐ 04	☐ 05
Contribution-related pay	☐ 01	☐ 02	☐ 03	☐ 04	☐ 05
Team pay	☐ 01	☐ 02	☐ 03	☐ 04	☐ 05
Coaching and/or mentoring	☐ 01	☐ 02	☐ 03	☐ 04	☐ 05
Career management and/or succession-planning	☐ 01	☐ 02	☐ 03	☐ 04	☐ 05
Personal development plans	☐ 01	☐ 02	☐ 03	☐ 04	☐ 05

Other (please specify) ....
....

3 **Are individual, team and organisational objectives linked?**

Yes ☐ 01   No ☐ 02

If yes, how are they linked? ....

....

....

4 Who sets the performance requirements for individuals? *(Please tick as many boxes as appropriate.)*

Senior managers ☐ 01   Line managers/team leaders ☐ 02   Personnel staff ☐ 03

Other *(please specify)* ☐ 04 ....

5 Are the current performance-management arrangements:

A new system (ie developed within the last two years)	☐ 01
A development of an older system	☐ 02
An old-established system	☐ 03
Other *(please specify)*	☐ 04 ....

....

6 How long did it take to develop the system?

Less than one year	☐ 01
More than one year but less than two years	☐ 02
More than two years	☐ 03

7 How long did it take to implement the system?

Less than one year	☐ 01
More than one year but less than two years	☐ 02
More than two years	☐ 03

8 Who was consulted regarding the development and design of the system? *(Please tick as many boxes as appropriate.)*

All Staff ☐ 01   Senior managers ☐ 02   Other managers/team leaders ☐ 03

TU officials ☐ 04   Staff representatives ☐ 05   Personnel staff ☐ 06

9 How did consultation take place?

Workforce representatives on advisory panels	☐ 01
Briefing sessions for groups of employees	☐ 02
Comments/information channel through line managers	☐ 03
Other *(please specify)*	☐ 04 ....

....

....

10 Who (if anybody) receives training in performance-management techniques? *(Please tick as many boxes as appropriate.)*

All staff ☐ 01   Appraisers ☐ 02   Head of department ☐ 03

Personnel staff ☐ 04   No one ☐ 05   Team leaders ☐ 06

SECTION D – PROCESS OF PERFORMANCE MANAGEMENT

1 To what extent do you agree that the following statements describe performance-management processes in your organisation?

	Strongly agree	Slightly agree	Slightly disagree	Strongly disagree
Pay contingent on performance is an essential part of performance management	☐ 01	☐ 02	☐ 03	☐ 04
Line managers own and operate the performance-management process	☐ 01	☐ 02	☐ 03	☐ 04
Performance management is an integrated part of the employee-line manager relationship	☐ 01	☐ 02	☐ 03	☐ 04
Performance management is integrated with other people-management processes	☐ 01	☐ 02	☐ 03	☐ 04
The focus of performance management is developmental	☐ 01	☐ 02	☐ 03	☐ 04
Performance management integrates the goals of individuals with those of the organisation	☐ 01	☐ 02	☐ 03	☐ 04
Performance management is an integral part of the people management strategy	☐ 01	☐ 02	☐ 03	☐ 04
Performance management motivates individuals	☐ 01	☐ 02	☐ 03	☐ 04
Performance management is used to manage organisational culture	☐ 01	☐ 02	☐ 03	☐ 04
Performance management sets stretching and challenging goals	☐ 01	☐ 02	☐ 03	☐ 04
Performance management is bureaucratic and time-consuming	☐ 01	☐ 02	☐ 03	☐ 04
The aims and objectives of performance management are well communicated and fully understood	☐ 01	☐ 02	☐ 03	☐ 04
Performance management helps us express the value of the people contribution in the organisation	☐ 01	☐ 02	☐ 03	☐ 04

2 Do you give an overall rating for performance?

Yes ☐ 01   No ☐ 02

If yes, what sort of categories do you use?

Numerical/alphabetical ☐ 01   Verbal (all positive) ☐ 02

Verbal (positive and negative) ☐ 03

Other *(please specify)* ☐ 04 ....

If you use numerical/alphabetical rating please indicate the number of levels used

3 ☐ 01   4 ☐ 02   5 ☐ 03   ☐ 04 6 or more

3 Do you use any of the following to achieve consistency in ratings across different parts of the organisation?

Forced distribution   ☐ 01

Management group review   ☐ 02

Points rating system   ☐ 03

Grandparenting system   ☐ 04

Prior estimates by management group   ☐ 05

Peer review of outcomes   ☐ 06

Standard-setting workshops or seminars   ☐ 07

Others *(please specify)*   ☐ 08 ....

....

4 Do you use performance-management ratings to inform contingent pay decisions?

Yes ☐ 01   No ☐ 02

If you do not use ratings, how are contingent pay decisions made?

....

....

....

If no, do you separate performance-management reviews from contingent pay reviews?

Yes ☐ 01   No ☐ 02

If yes, how long is the period of separation?

1 to 3 months ☐ 01   3–6 months ☐ 02   longer than 6 months ☐ 03

5 To what extent do you believe you have buy-in from line managers about your performance-management processes?

Most are completely and actively in favour   ☐ 01

Most generally accept that it us useful   ☐ 02

Many are indifferent to performance
management but go through the motions   ☐ 03

Many are hostile to performance management   ☐ 04

6 Who keeps the documentation?

Personnel department ☐ 01　　Line manager ☐ 02　　Individual ☐ 03

Other *(please specify)* ☐ 04　...

SECTION E – PERFORMANCE MANAGEMENT OUTCOMES

1 Is there a formal system for the evaluation of performance management?

Yes ☐ 01　　　No ☐ 02

If yes, please specify the process you use to evaluate

Opinion/attitude surveys	☐ 01
Focus groups	☐ 02
Informal feedback (verbal)	☐ 03
Formal feedback (written)	☐ 04

Other *(please specify)* ☐ 05　...

....

2 How important are the following criteria in the measurement of individual performance in organisation?

	Very important	Important	Not very important	Not used as a measure
Customer Care	☐ 01	☐ 02	☐ 03	☐ 04
Quality	☐ 01	☐ 02	☐ 03	☐ 04
Flexibility	☐ 01	☐ 02	☐ 03	☐ 04
Competence	☐ 01	☐ 02	☐ 03	☐ 04
Skills/learning targets	☐ 01	☐ 02	☐ 03	☐ 04
Business awareness	☐ 01	☐ 02	☐ 03	☐ 04
Working relationships	☐ 01	☐ 02	☐ 03	☐ 04
Contribution to team	☐ 01	☐ 02	☐ 03	☐ 04
Financial awareness	☐ 01	☐ 02	☐ 03	☐ 04
Productivity	☐ 01	☐ 02	☐ 03	☐ 04
Aligning personal objectives with organisational goals	☐ 01	☐ 02	☐ 03	☐ 04
Achievement of objectives	☐ 01	☐ 02	☐ 03	☐ 04

3 How is the performance management system regarded by

	Very effective	Moderately effective	Effective	Not very effective
Senior managers	☐ 01	☐ 02	☐ 03	☐ 04
Other managers/team leaders	☐ 01	☐ 02	☐ 03	☐ 04
Other staff	☐ 01	☐ 02	☐ 03	☐ 04
Personnel	☐ 01	☐ 02	☐ 03	☐ 04

4 Are you proposing to make any changes to your performance-management arrangements over the next 12 months?

Yes ☐ 01   No ☐ 02   Don't know ☐ 03

5 What are the key factors which you use to determine whether performance management is effective? *(Please rank the relevant factors only in order of importance, with 1 being most important.)*

Achievement of financial targets	☐ 01	Productivity	☐ 06
Development of skills	☐ 02	Development of competence	☐ 07
Improved customer care	☐ 03	Improved quality	☐ 08
Changes in behaviour	☐ 04	Changes in attitude	☐ 09
Motivation	☐ 05	Labour turnover	☐ 10
Other *(please specify)*	☐ 11	....	

....

6 In general, how effective have your organisation's performance-management processes proved in improving overall performance?

Very effective ☐ 01   Moderately effective ☐ 02   Effective ☐ 03
Ineffective ☐ 04   Don't know ☐ 05

7 Can you summarise three key issues which you believe are important in the introduction, maintenance or improvement of performance management

1 ....
....

2 ....
....

3 ....
....

Performance Management Bibliography

ADVISORY, CONCILIATION AND ARBITRATION SERVICE (1988) *Employee Appraisal.* London, ACAS.

ANTONIONI, D. (1994) 'Improve the performance management process before discontinuing performance appraisals'. *Compensation & Benefits Review.* May–June, pp.29–37.

ARGYRIS, C. (1992) *On Organisational Learning.* Cambridge, Mass., Blackwell.

AUDIT COMMISSION (1987) *Performance Review in Local Government.*

BAGULEY, P. (1994) *Improving Organisational Performance.* Maidenhead, McGraw-Hill.

BAILEY, R. T. (1983) *Measurement of Performance.* Aldershot, Gower.

BARLOW, G. (1989) 'Deficiencies and the perpetuation of power: latent functions in performance appraisal'. *Journal of Management Studies.* September, pp.499–517.

BATES, R. A. *and* HOLTON, E. F. (1995) 'Computerised performance monitoring: a review of human resource issues'. *Human Resource Management Review.* Winter, pp.267–288.

BATES, S. (2003) 'Forced ranking'. *HR Magazine.* June, pp.65–68.

BEAVER, G. a*nd* HARRIS, L. (1995) 'Performance management and the small firm: dilemmas, tensions and paradoxes'. *Journal of Strategic Change.* Vol. 4, pp.109–119.

BEER, M. *and* RUH, R. A. (1976) 'Employee growth through performance management'. *Harvard Business Review.* July–August, pp.59–66.

BERNADIN, H. K., KANE, J. S., ROSS, S., SPINA, J. D. *and* JOHNSON, D. L. (1995) 'Performance appraisal design, development and implementation', in G. R. Ferris, S. D. Rosen, and D. J. Barnum (eds), *Handbook of Human Resource Management.* Cambridge Mass., Blackwell.

BEVAN, S. *and* THOMPSON, M. (1991) 'Performance management at the crossroads'. *Personnel Management.* November, pp.36–39.

BITICI, U. S., CARRIE, A. S. a*nd* McDEVITT, L. (1997) 'Integrate performance management systems: an audit and development goal'. *The TQM Magazine.* Vol. 9 No. 1, pp.46–53.

BOWLES, M. L. *and* COATES, G. (1993) 'Image and substance: the management of performance as rhetoric or reality?' *Personnel Review.* Vol. 22 No. 2, pp.3–21.

BOYATZIS, R. (1982) *The Competent Manager.* New York, Wiley.

BOYETT, J. H. *and* CONN, H. P. (1995) *Maximum Performance Management.* Oxford, Glenbridge Publishing.

BRANCATO, C. K. (1995) *New Corporate Performance Measures,* New York, The Conference Board.

BRUMBACH, G. B. (1988) 'Some ideas, issues and predictions about performance management'. *Public Personnel Management.* Winter, pp.387–402.

CAMPBELL, J. P. (1990) 'Modelling the performance prediction problem in industrial and organizational psychology', in M. P. Dunnette and L. M. Hugh (eds), *Handbook of Industrial and Organizational Psychology.* Cambridge Mass., Blackwell.

CARDY, R. L. *and* DOBBINS, G. H. (1994) *Performance Appraisal: Alternative Perspectives.* Cincinnati, Ohio, South-Western Publishing.

CARLTON, I. *and* SLOMAN, M. (1992) 'Performance appraisal in practice.' *Human Resource Management Journal.* Vol. 2 No. 3, Spring, pp.80–94.

CONE, J. W. *and* ROBINSON, D. G. (2001) 'The power of performance'. *TD.* August, pp.32–41.

DANIIELS, A. C. (1987) 'What is PM?' *Performance Management.* July, pp.8–12.

DEMING, W. E. (1986) *Out of the Crisis.* Cambridge, Mass., Massachusetts Institute of Technology. Center for Advanced Engineering Studies.

DRUCKER, P. (1955) *The Practice of Management.* London, Heinemann.

EARLEY, D. C. (1986) 'Computer-generated performance feedback in the magazine industry'. *Organisation Behaviour and Human Decision Processes.* Vol. 41, pp.50–64.

EDWARDS, M. R. *and* EWEN, A. T. (1996) *360-degree Feedback.* New York, American Management Association.

EDWARDS, M. R., EWEN, A. T. *and* O'NEAL, S. (1994) 'Using multi-source assessment to pay people not jobs'. *ACA Journal.* Summer, pp.6–17.

EGAN, G. (1995) 'A clear path to peak performance'. *People Management.* 18 May, pp.34–37.

ENGELMANN, C. H. *and* ROESCH, C. H. (1996) *Managing Individual Performance.* Scottsdale, Ariz., American Compensation Association.

EPSTEIN, S. *and* O'BRIEN, E. J. 'The person-situation debate in historical perspective'. *Psychological Bulletin.* Vol. 83, pp.956–974.

FISHER, C. M. (1994) 'The difference between appraisal schemes: variation and acceptability – part 1'. *Personnel Review.* Vol. 23 No. 8, pp.33–48.

FISHER, M. (1995) *Performance Appraisals.* London, Kogan Page.

FLANAGAN, J. C (1954) 'The critical incident technique'. *Psychological Bulletin.* Vol. 51, pp.327–358.

FLETCHER, C. (1993a) *Appraisal: Routes to Improved Performance.* London, Institute of Personnel and Development.

FLETCHER, C. (1993b) 'Appraisal: an idea whose time has gone?' *Personnel Management*, September, pp.34–37.

FLETCHER, C. *and* WILLIAMS, R. (1992) 'Organisational experience'. in *Performance Management in the UK: An Analysis of the Issues*. London, Institute of Personnel and Development.

FOWLER, A. (1990) 'Performance management; the MBO of the '90s?' *Personnel Management*. July, pp.47–54.

FOWLER, A. (1995) *The Disciplinary Interview*. London, Institute of Personnel and Development.

FURNHAM, A. (1996) 'Starved of feedback'. *The Independent*. 5 December.

GANNON, M. (1995) 'Personal development planning', in M. Walters (ed.), *The Performance Management Handbook*. London, Institute of Personnel and Development.

GEORGE, J. (1986) 'Appraisal in the public sector: dispensing with the big stick'. *Personnel Management*. May, pp.32–35.

GOODRIDGE, M. (2001) 'The limits of performance management'. *Topics 3*. ER Consultants, pp.23–28.

GRINT, K. (1993) 'What's wrong with performance appraisal? A critique and a suggestion'. *Human Resource Management Journal*. Spring, pp.61–77.

GROSS, S. E. (1995) *Compensation for Teams*. New York, Hay.

GUIN, K. A. (1992) *Successfully Integrating Total Quality and Performance Appraisal*. New York, Spring, Faulkner and Gray.

HAMPSON, S. E. (1982) *The Construction of Personality*. London, Routledge.

HANDY, L., DEVINE, M. *and* HEATH, L. (1996) *360-degree feedback: Unguided Missile or Powerful Weapon?* Berkhamsted, Ashridge Management Group.

HARRISON, R. (1997) *Employee Development*. 2nd edn. London, Institute of Personnel and Development.

HARTLE, F. (1995) *Transforming the Performance Management Process*. London, Kogan Page.

HENDRY, C., BRADLEY, P. *and* PERKINS, S. (1997) 'Missed'. *People Management*. 15 May, pp.20–25.

HERZBERG, F. (1968) 'One more time: how do you motivate your employees?' *Harvard Business Review*. Jan–Feb, pp.109–120.

HUMBLE, J. (1972) *Management by Objectives*. London, Management Publications.

IDS STUDY No. 626 (1997) *Performance Management*. London, Incomes Data Services. May.

INDUSTRIAL SOCIETY (1996) *Managing Best practice: Rewarding performance*. London, Industrial Society.

INSTITUTE OF PERSONNEL MANAGEMENT (1992) *Performance Management in the UK: an analysis of the issues*. London.

JONES, P., PALMER, J., WHITEHEAD, D. *and* NEEDHAM, P. (1995) 'Prisms of performance'. *The Ashridge Journal*. April, pp.10–14.

JONES, T. W. (1995) 'Performance management in a changing context'. *Human Resource Management.* Fall, pp.425–442.

KANE, J. S. (1996) 'The conceptualisation and representation of total performance effectiveness'. *Human Resource Management Review.* Summer, pp.123–145.

KAPLAN, R. S. *and* NORTON, D. P. (1992) 'The balanced scorecard – measures that drive performance'. *Harvard Business Review.* Jan–Feb, pp.71–79.

KAPLAN, R. S. *and* NORTON, D. P. (1996a) 'Using the balanced scorecard as a strategic management system'. *Harvard Business Review.* Jan–Feb, pp.75–85.

KAPLAN, R. S. *and* NORTON, D. P. (1996b) 'Strategic learning and the balanced scorecard'. *Strategy and Leadership.* June, pp.20–34.

KEARNS, P. (2000) 'How do you measure up?' *Personnel Today.* 21 March, pp.21–22.

KERMALLY. S. (1997) *Managing Performance.* Oxford, Butterworth-Heinemann.

KESSLER, I. *and* PURCELL, J. (1992) 'Performance-related pay: objectives and application'. *Human Resource Management.* Spring, pp.16–33.

LATHAM, G. P. *and* LOCKE, E. A. (1979) 'Goal Setting – a motivational technique that works'. *Organisational Dynamics.* Autumn, pp.442–447.

LAWLER, E. E. *and* McDERMOTT, M. (2003) 'Current performance management practices'. *WorldatWork Journal.* Second Quarter, pp.49–60.

LAWSON, P. (1995) 'Performance management: an overview', in M. Walters (ed.), *The Performance Management Handbook.* London, Institute of Personnel and Development.

LAZER, R. I. *and* WIKSTROM. W. S. (1977) *Appraising Managerial Performance: Current Practices and New Directions.* New York, The Conference Board.

LEVENTHAL, G. S. (1980) 'What should be done with equity theory? New approaches to the study of fairness in social relationships', in K. Gerken, M. Greenberg, R. Willis (eds), *Social Exchange: Advances in Theory and Research.* New York, Plenum Press.

LEVINSON, H. (1970) 'Management by whose objectives?' *Harvard Business Review.* July–August, pp.125–134.

LEVINSON, H. (1976) 'Appraisal of *what* performance?' *Harvard Business Review.* July–August, pp.30–46.

LOCAL GOVERNMENT MANAGEMENT BOARD (1995) *Guide to 360-degree feedback.*

LOCKETT, J. (1992) *Effective Performance Management.* London, Kogan Page.

LONDON, M. *and* BEATTY, R. W. (1993) '360-degree feedback as competitive advantage'. *Human Resource Management.* Summer/Fall, pp.353–372.

LONG, P. (1986) *Performance Appraisal Revisited.* London, Institute of Personnel Management.

MACKCAY, I. (1992) A *Manager's Guide to the Appraisal Discussion.* London, BACIE.

MAIER, N. (1958)*The Appraisal Interview.* New York, Wiley.

McDONALD, D. and SMITH, A. (1991) 'A proven connection: performance management and business results'. *Compensation & Benefits Review.* January–February, pp.59–64.

McGREGOR, D. (1957) 'An uneasy look at performance appraisal'. *Harvard Business Review.* May–June, pp.89–94.

MARCHINGTON, M. *and* WILKINSON, A. (1996) *Core Personnel and Development.* London, Institute of personnel and Development.

MEISLER, A. (2003) 'Dead man's curve'. *Workforce Management.* June, pp.44–49.

MILKOVICH, G. and WIGDOR, A. C. (1991) *Pay for Performance: Evaluating Performance Appraisal and Merit Pay.* Washington, DC, National Academy Press.

MOHRMAN, A. M. *and* MOHRMAN, S. A. (1995) 'Performance management is "running the business"'. *Compensation & Benefits Review.* July–August, pp.69–75.

MUMFORD, A. (1989) *Management Development: Strategies for Action.* London, Institute of Personnel Management.

MURPHY, K. *and* CLEVELAND, J. (1995) *Understanding Performance Appraisal.* London, Sage.

NALBANTIAN, HAIG R., GUZZO, RICHARD A., KIEFFER, DAVE *and* DOHERTY, JAY (2004) *Play to Your Strengths.* New York, McGraw-Hill.

NEELY, A., GRAY, D., KENNEDY, M. *and* MARR, B. (2002) *Measuring Corporate Management and Leadership Capability.* London, Council for Excellence in Management and Leadership.

 NEWTON, T. and FINDLAY, P. (1996) 'Playing God?: the performance of appraisal'. *Human Resource Management Journal.* Vol. 6 No. 3, pp.42–56.

OAKLAND, J. S. (1993) *Total Quality Management: The Route to Improved Performance.* 2nd edn. Oxford, Butterworth-Heinemann.

PEARCE, J. A. *and* ROBINSON, R. B. (1988) *Strategic Management: Strategy Formulation and Implementation.* Georgetown, Ontario, Irwin.

PEDLER, M., BURGOYNE, J. *and* BOYDELL, T. (1986) *Manager's Guide to Self Development.* 2nd edn. Maidenhead, McGraw-Hill.

PHILPOTT, L. *and* SHEPPARD, L. (1992) 'Managing for improved performance', in Michael Armstrong (ed.), *Strategies for Human Resource Management.* London, Kogan Page.

PLACHY, R. J *and* PLACHY, S. J. (1988) *Getting Results From Your Performance Management and Appraisal System.* New York, AMACOM.

PORTER, L. W. *and* LAWLER, E. E. *Managerial Attitudes and Performance.* Homewood, Ill., Irwin Dorsey.

RANDELL, G. H. (1973) 'Performance appraisal: purpose, practices and conflicts'. *Occupational Psychology.* Vol. 47, pp.221–224.

ROBERTSON, I. T., SMITH, M. *and* COOPER, C. L. (1992) *Motivation.* London, Institute of Personnel and Development.

ROWE, K. (1964) 'An appraisal of appraisals'. *Journal of Management Studies.* Vol. 1 No. 1, March, pp.1–25.

RUCCI, A. J., KIRN, S. P. *and* QUINN, R. T. (1998) 'The employee-customer-profit chain at Sears'. *Harvard Business Review.* January–February, pp.82–97.

SCHAFFER, R. H. (1991) 'Demand better results and get them'. *Harvard Business Review.* March–April, pp.142–149.

SHNEIDERMAN, A. M. (1999), 'Why balanced score cards fail'. *Journal of Strategic Performance Measurement.* January, pp.6–10

SPARROW, P. (1996) 'Too good to be true'. *People Management.* 5 December, pp.22–27.

SPENCER, L. *and* SPENCER, S. (1993) *Competence at Work.* New York, Wiley.

STEWART, V. a*nd* STEWART, A. (1982) *Managing the Poor Performer.* Aldershot, Gower.

STILES, P., GRATTON, L. *and* TRUSS, C. (1997) 'Performance management and the psychological contract'. *Human Resource Management Journal.* Vol. 2 No. 1, pp.57–66.

STOREY, J. (1985) 'The means of management control'. *Sociology.* Vol. 19 No. 2, pp.193–212.

SWANSON, R. A. (1994) *Analysing for Improved Performance,* New York, Berrett-Koelher.

TAMKIN, P., BARBER, L. *and* HIRSH, W. (1995) *Personal Development Plans: Case Studies of Practice.* Brighton, The Institute for Employment Studies.

THOMAS, C. (1995) 'Performance management'. *Croner Pay and Benefits Bulletin.* August, pp.4–5.

THOR, G. G. (1995) 'Using measurement to reinforce strategy', in H. Rishner and C. Fay (eds), *The Performance Imperative.* San Fransisco, Jossey Bass.

TOWNLEY, B. (1990) 'A discriminating approach to appraisal'. *Personnel Management.* December, pp.34–37.

TOWNLEY, B. (1990/1991) 'Appraisal into UK universities'. *Human Resource Management Journal.* Vol. 1 No. 2, pp.27–44

TURNOW, W. W. (1993) 'Introduction to special issue on 360-degree feedback'. *Human Resource Management.* Summer/Fall, pp.311–316.

van de VLIET, A. (1997) 'The new balancing card'. *Management Today.* July, pp.78–79.

WALTERS, M. (1995a) *The Performance Management Handbook.* London, Institute of Personnel and Development.

WALTERS, M. (1995b) 'Developing organisational measures', in M. Walters (ed.), *The Performance Management Handbook.* London, Institute of Personnel and Development.

WARD, P. (1997) *360-Degree Feedback.* London, Institute of Personnel and Development.

WHEATLEY, M. (1996) 'How to score performance management'. *Human Resources.* May–June, pp.24–26.

WICK, C. W. *and* LEON, L. S. (1995) 'Creating a learning organisation: from ideas to action'. *Human Resource Management.* Summer, pp.299–311.

WILLIAMS, S. (1991) 'Strategy and objectives', in, F. Neale (ed.) *The Handbook of Performance Management.* London, Institute of Personnel and Development.

WINSTANLEY, D. *and* STUART-SMITH, K. (1996) 'Policing performance: the ethics of performance management'. *Personnel Review.* Vol. 25 No. 6, pp.66–84.

ZIGON, J. (1994) 'Measuring the performance of work teams'. *ACA Journal.* Autumn, pp.18–32.

Index